HAMPTON COURT
The story of a village

Gerald Heath

Edited by
Kathy White and Joan Heath

THE HAMPTON COURT ASSOCIATION

Cover: *The First Grand Match of Cricket played by Members of the Royal Amateur Society on Hampton Court Green*, 1836. British School, nineteenth century

Reproduced by kind permission of the Yale Center for British Art, Paul Mellon Collection

First published 2000 by the Hampton Court Association
Paddock Lodge, The Green, Hampton Court, KT8 9BW

© 2000 by Kathy White and Joan Heath

The right of Kathy White and Joan Heath to be identified as the owners
of this work has been asserted by them in accordance with the
Copyright, Design and Patents Act 1988

British Library Cataloguing in Publication Data
A catalogue record for this book is available from the British Library

ISBN 0-9538700-0-6

Printed and bound by Redwood Books Limited, Trowbridge, Wiltshire

Contents

Acknowledgements

The Editors are grateful to Peter Foster
for his additional research and contribution.

Thanks for practical advice and contributions are many
and due especially to Gill Heath, John Kitchin, Peggy
Fonge, Diana Bayne, John Sheaf, Les Strudwick,
Jonathan Foyle, Clare Murphy, Vivienne Andrews,
Matthew Allchurch, Mark Wilding, Lynne Ferguson, John
Horne, Colin White, Melissa Gold, Ilsa Yardley, Anne
Coles and to the residents of the village of Hampton Court
for their enthusiasm and support.

Foreword

When members of the Hampton Court Association gathered for our 1999 New Year Party to discuss how to celebrate the Millennium we were in the midst of an acute identity crisis.

According to the postal authorities we live in Surrey although we pay our rates to Richmond-upon-Thames which is part of Greater London. We live north of the Thames but our official address is East Molesey on the opposite side of the river. We have been allocated Kingston post-codes which only serve to confuse the drivers of delivery vans and others trying to locate our homes. And in discussion with appropriate authorities we are told that 'Hampton Court' is not a recognised address.

The gathering agreed it was high time we reclaimed our past. This could be our Millennium project, to re-establish our identity. Hampton Court, after all, is a name of great antiquity which had been in existence well over a century before the building of the Palace. There must be a story here which would be worth exploring. As we raised our glasses to that proposal, we had little idea that someone had got there before us.

Gerald Heath, a distinguished local historian, had in fact been working for several years before his death on a history which he called 'the village of Hampton Court'. It was a startling concept and could be read alongside a history of the Palace although at the same time it opened up new areas of research which most of those histories had ignored. Sadly, Gerald never completed it although what he had already written was enough to expand into a fascinating and original book.

It is to Gerald's widow, Joan Heath, that we owe a debt of gratitude for making this material available and who also offered to work on the editing with Kathy White – author (with Peter Foster) of a history of Bushy Park – who volunteered to undertake the task of carrying out the revision, research and necessary additions to complete the text.

Since this was to be a community project, everyone in the area was circulated with requests for information about their own houses. An application was successfully submitted for a grant from the Millennium Awards for All. The result is this handsome volume which I know will be read with special interest by local people, but will also, I believe, fascinate the wider public for whom the name Hampton Court indicates only the Palace.

The story of the village is, of course, inextricable from the Palace. One would not exist without the other. But the emphasis here is different. The Palace story centres on the kings and queens who lived in it. Here the reader will encounter the artisans, craftsmen and officials, the people who actually built and served it over the centuries and made their homes here. Some, like Sir Christopher Wren, 'Capability' Brown and Jean Tijou, will be familiar; others, like Andrew Snape who built an inn near the ferry, or James Turner, who was forced to close his butcher's shop after complaints from the village doctor, are less well remembered. You will also meet the redoubtable Princess Sophia Duleep Singh, daughter of the last ruler of the Punjab, who outraged local opinion as the dedicated leader of the local branch of the Women's Suffragist campaign.

Finally the reader will be left in little doubt that Hampton Court means much more than a royal palace. If a true history of Oxford must include 'Town' as well as 'Gown', so this story of the village is a blend of contrasting but intermingled elements which weave through the centuries and together make up the history of Hampton Court.

Louis Marks
Chairman
The Hampton Court Association
August, 2000

Map 1 *Hampton Court Village and its surrounds*

Extract from 'Survey of the County of Middlesex' by John Rocque, 1754

COURT VILLAGE, HAMPTON COURT.

'Court Village, Hampton Court' from corner of The Green to Bushy Park entrance with shops and tearooms, circa 1904. The collection of L. Strudwick

Introduction

This is the history of a village which has never in its whole existence had any official status. The visitor approaching the Palace of Hampton Court from Hampton or Hampton Wick will see signposts announcing Hampton Court, but the village has no boundaries recognised by any map-maker. It does not exist as far as local government is concerned, but historically and topographically it is, and always has been, quite distinct from the two parishes and electoral wards to which it is bound. Yet it is this community which is the true village of Hampton Court.

The village has been almost entirely neglected in historical and topographical literature, presumably because it is overshadowed in importance and interest by the Palace, which has been fully dealt with by many authors, especially by Ernest Law, whose *History of Hampton Court Palace*, published between 1885 and 1898, has so well stood the test of time. It cannot be doubted, however, that if Hampton Court Village existed in isolation, it would be noted for its spacious Green, for the architecture of many of its buildings, and for the company of distinguished men and women who have lived there. Tribute must also be paid to the many craftsmen who have lived and worked in the village, whose names are for the most part unknown to the world at large, but who, by their special skills, helped to create the buildings, gardens and parks we admire today.

It is the aim of this book to fill the gap by recording the history of the village that is bounded on the north by Bushy Park, on the south by the River Thames and the walls of the Palace and Home Park, on the west by Hampton-on-Thames, and on the east by Hampton Wick. It comprises The Green and the buildings which border it, the approach to Hampton Court Bridge, Frog Walk, the road from Hampton Court towards Hampton, and the road from Hampton Court to Hampton Wick, known for four hundred years and more as 'Between the Walls', the walls, that is, of the Royal Parks. The buildings which stand, or used to stand, in Outer Green Court, between the Trophy Gates and the Palace have also been included as they too were on the outer side of the moat and outside the Palace proper; moreover they have been given hardly any attention until now, even by Ernest Law. For like reasons Wilderness House has also been included, although it is manifestly within the Palace walls.

Cramped as it is between boundaries of royal demesne and river, Hampton Court Village must be unique among British villages in having been incapable of expanding into the countryside around it. This has meant that its development could only take place by encroachment on a very small area of common land or by building anew on the sites of old houses.

The small community of Hampton Court Village straddles two parishes – that of St Mary, Hampton, on the west, and that of St John, Hampton Wick on the east. The original parish of St Mary covered the town of Hampton and the hamlet of Hampton Wick (wick in this instance signifying hamlet), but the Wick had its own churchwarden at least as early as 1653. From 1661 onwards there was constant friction between them over the sum of £11 10s alleged to be owed to the Town by the Wick. When the Wick refused to pay, the Town retaliated by withholding the Wick's entitlement to one-third of the income from the parish charities. Feeling was so intense that the Wick officers took legal proceedings against the Town in 1681, to the disadvantage of the parishioners, who had to pay the legal expenses, and who gained nothing from the case. A formal agreement was entered into in 1698 whereby the Wick paid the £11 10s claimed by the Town and the Town restored the payment of the charity money, but this proved to be a short-lived truce and causes for dispute were found for another 134 years.

In 1764 the Wick again engaged in legal proceedings against the Town, from which the only ones to gain were the gentlemen of the law. Hampton Wick's opportunity came when St Mary's church had either to be extended or rebuilt, and in 1831 both sides agreed that the most acceptable solution would be to form two separate parishes, the areas of which were to be in the time-honoured proportion of two to the Town and one to the Wick, which gave rise to a whimsically tortuous boundary line. In the division Hampton retained the Palace, but allowed to Hampton Wick the Tennis Court, the Tiltyard and the Wilderness.

The next stage in the separation of Hampton Wick from Hampton came after the passing of the Local Government Act of 1858, which enabled Hampton Wick to set up its own Local Board in 1863. Hampton, on the other hand, resolutely refused to adopt the Act and maintained the old system of government by vestry, churchwardens, surveyors of the highways and overseers of the poor until 1890, when a Local Board was at last formed. In 1863 half of the residents of Hampton Court Village, those who lived 'Between the Walls', found themselves governed by the Hampton Wick Local Board, whereas the remainder were tied by Hampton's adherence to the old system. In 1865, when the advantages of the new system were becoming apparent, those in the Hampton part of the village attempted to have the boundary changed so that they could become part of Hampton Wick, but they had no success, and so had to wait until 1890, when the Hampton Local Board came into being. The division of Hampton Court Village into two parts lost most of its significance in 1937, when both the Hampton and the Hampton Wick Urban District Councils, which had replaced the Local Boards in 1895, were assimilated into the new Borough of Twickenham, the main distinction being the continuation of the two districts as electoral wards although the ward boundary for Hampton was extended to the entrance of Bushy Park. Finally, on the passing of the Greater London Council Act (1964), Hampton Court Village became a part of the new Borough of Richmond-upon-Thames.

Most of Hampton Court Village had once been servile land, held by 'copy of Court Roll' instead of tenure directly from the King. Copyhold land by origin was land that had once been occupied by serfs, owing the manorial lord their work to cultivate the manor farmland. Grants of waste land on copyhold tenure were made from time to time by the Manor Court to officials of the Royal Household or of the government as a perquisite of office, and were subject only to the payment of a fine on admission and an annual quit rent, rarely more than a shilling or two, for the benefit of the poor of Hampton or Hampton Wick.

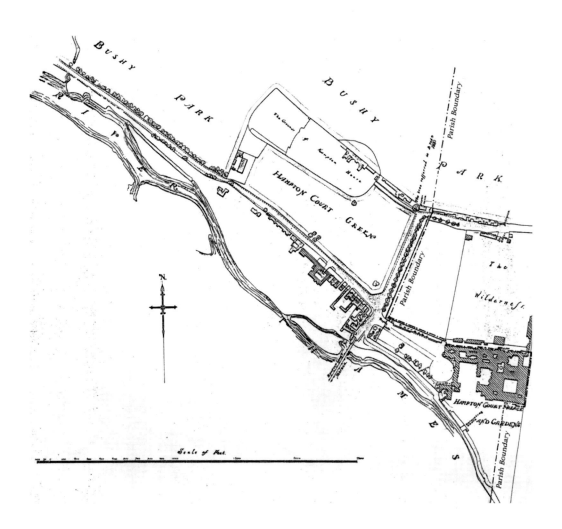

Map 2 *The two parishes of Hampton Court Village. The boundary line passed round the south and east fronts of the Palace, through the wall and down Tennis Court Lane (where it is still marked by a stone set in the wall), behind the old barrack block, along the inside of the wall of Frog Walk (sometimes known as Vrow Walk) and through the wall at the end, over the road to what used to be a restaurant, then the office of an archery company and now a private house and so into Bushy Park. At the beating of the bounds of the parishes, some of the more agile participants, after twice scaling the walls of the Palace, used to pass through the restaurant and out through the kitchen window into Bushy Park.* Extract from 'Plan of the Roads in the Parish of Hampton', 1877

Hampton Court Village does not conform to the usual pattern of a village, either administratively or topographically. As far as local government, law enforcement, poor relief, public services and communications are concerned, its history is part of the history of Hampton and of Hampton Wick. It had come into being between 1514 and 1538 as the operational base for the building of the Palace, and reached its apogee as a village with the rebuilding of the Palace between 1689 and 1702. Its economic history is almost entirely concerned with the provision of homes and working places for the royal servants who built and maintained the Palace, and of accommodation and services for visitors to the Palace, at first to attend the Court there, and later to enjoy it as a magnificent national monument. Its religious history, apart from the holding of Nonconformist services at Glycine House for a brief period in the 1870s, is shared between the churches of St Mary, Hampton, St John, Hampton Wick, and the Chapel Royal. As far as recreation is concerned, sports clubs based on Hampton Court Village have had a spasmodic existence; and social activities were usually held in the hotels and inns.

The history told here is for the most part that of the builders of the Palace, the tenants of the Crown, their homes, their inns, their shops, and their use of the common land, Hampton Court Green, for work, recreation, or military purposes. The earlier histories of some of the buildings are traced in the Appendix. There are now no copyholders – between the 1850s and 1922 all copyhold leases were converted to freeholds.

CHAPTER I

The Early Village

So far no trace has been found of any settlement in the region of Hampton Court earlier than the Bronze Age. The only barrow known to have existed in the area, lying not far from the northern end of the Chestnut Avenue in Bushy Park, was excavated in 1854. There is likewise little evidence of Saxon life around Hampton Court, the only discovered artefacts being a few weapons dredged from the bed of the Thames in the late nineteenth and early twentieth centuries. The Domesday Book, however, confirms the existence of a manor of Hampton before the Norman Conquest belonging to a Saxon named Aelfgar who was Earl of Mercia. The left bank of the Thames from Kempton to Brentford had been a Mercian possession for centuries. From the Dark Ages, Hampton never had a manor lord in residence and had been run for the benefit of absentee landlords. Certainly Earl Aelfgar never lived there.

The name 'Hampton' is considered to be derived from the Saxon words 'hamn' meaning 'a bend in the river' and 'ton' – 'a fortified place'; and a bend in the river still today is a prominent feature.

The Domesday Survey, being primarily concerned with land valuation, gives no information regarding houses or other buildings. If the assumed derivation of the name Hampton is correct, there must have been some form of manorial enclave and it is likely that it would have been located not too far from the village of Hampton.

After the Conquest the manor was granted by King William I to the Norman lord, Walter de St Valerie, and it remained in his family until about 1217, when Thomas de St Valerie was exiled and the manor of Hampton became the property of a London merchant, Henry de St Albans. Some years later it was acquired by the Knights Hospitaller of St John of Jerusalem in England. The Hospitallers already owned sheep pastures about a mile from the village of Hampton, now part of Home Park. It is likely their small house or 'camera', which was one of many held by their Order throughout England, stood on the site which is now Hampton Court Palace. After the manor was transferred from Henry de St Albans, the Hospitallers would naturally transfer the administrative centre of the manor to their own establishment from wherever it had been previously located.

The Hospitallers seem to have lived a peaceful, industrious and uneventful life at Hampton. It was very rarely that their name appeared in legal or administrative documents. On one occasion, in 1246, there was a dispute over the ownership of a few swans, and in 1288 the Preceptor was charged with harbouring a suspected murderer.

'Hampton Court' was in use as a place name as early as 1399 and was probably used to denote the demesne lands some 130 years before the King became lord of the manor. In

1476 John Wode, described as 'of Hampton Court' was appointed by King Edward IV 'to survey the River Thames and hear and determine offences against the ordinance of Magna Carta concerning the erection of weirs, mills, stanks (pools), piles and kiddles (stake fences) and other impediments'.

The camera also seems to have formed a sort of annexe to Shene Palace, the King's favourite palace at Richmond. In 1353 King Edward III stayed in the camera and some of his household accidentally burnt down some barns and other buildings, which the King caused to be rebuilt at his own expense.

Later, Hampton Court became popular with Henry VII when fire destroyed Richmond Palace in December 1497. The King's household still moved regularly from place to place and Richmond was one of the stops on its itinerary. When the palace there was no longer available, Hampton Court was a good nearby alternative.

In 1500 the King's Lord Chamberlain, Sir Giles Daubeney, emparked 300 acres of arable, the nucleus of Bushy Park, and was given a lease of 'Hamptoncourte' in 1505 for ninety-nine years. He died three years later and the lease was transferred to his wife who was not much interested and gave it up. In 1514 an ambitious Tudor statesman negotiated a new lease from the Hospitallers. The powerful Cardinal Wolsey was about to embark on one of the most significant building projects of the time.

CHAPTER II

Wolsey's Palace and the Village

When the Hospitallers leased their manor to Thomas Wolsey, Archbishop of York, for ninety-nine years the rent was £50 per annum. The terms of the lease allowed Wolsey and his assigns to 'take down, alter, transpose, chaunge, make and new byeld at theire propre costes any howses, walles, mootes, diches, warkis or other things within or about the seid manour of hamptoncourte . . .' Wolsey lost no time in demolishing the camera, except for the chapel, and in building for himself a house larger than any of Henry VIII's palaces. In Wolsey's building accounts for 1515 there are payments for repairs to the chapel, showing that he must have used the Hospitallers' chapel for a time before rebuilding it or building a new one. It is generally accepted that the new house arose on or near the site of the old camera and that the new chapel was built where the camera chapel had been, that is to say, on the ground which had already been consecrated.

The amount of information regarding the building of Wolsey's house is lamentably small. The little that remains is in the form of brief fortnightly accounts covering the year 1515. These give little more than a list of wages paid and materials purchased, from Kingston in many instances. From these accounts, however, it can be inferred that a substantial amount of building had been done during 1514, because by January 1515 many of the purchases related to the planting of the gardens, and a glazier was at work before the end of March of that year.

The pay-roll was a fairly large one, about one hundred, consisting mainly of masons, bricklayers, carpenters, sawyers, plasterers and labourers. The more skilled of these, and the masons in particular, were recruited by conscription from considerable distances away. So, while the building was in progress, there were many strangers in the neighbourhood, for whom lodgings had to be found and it is probable that accommodation for some of these had to be found in Molesey and other villages nearby as living space in Hampton and the Wick must have been stretched to the limit.

By July 1515 a wharf had been built to receive the materials. Watermen and labourers worked from sunrise to sunset to transport and distribute cargoes of stone, brick, timber, lime and plaster. The building must have proceeded at a good pace, because Wolsey was able to entertain Henry VIII and his Queen in his new house in May 1516 where they stayed in a suite of rooms designed for their sole use. In 1517 Wolsey paid for the making of a new moat round the house.

Provisions for this huge army of workmen as well as for the Cardinal's large household of 500 retainers were bought locally heralding a time of prosperity for the local community. Goods purchased at Kingston Market were sent by river to Hampton Court although the pressure on transport meant that carters were also employed.

Wolsey's vast new building was always short of water. When the Hospitallers had lived in the camera this was not a problem: water for its few inhabitants to drink could be dipped from the Thames or, more likely, from wells. The problem came when Wolsey was given the lease of Hampton Court. The number of people using the house rose dramatically and so did their need for water. In addition there were the ornamental ponds associated with the new gardens, dug in 1518. These were at first just dry holes in the ground; labourers had to ladle water out of the Thames at night to fill them.

Two springs served the palace. One conduit head was in what is now Bushy Park and the other local conduit had its head at Hampton, where the modern Plevna Road meets Thames Street. From it another wooden pipe ran alongside the Hampton Court Road to the Palace. Both conduit heads were brick built with windows and doors.

A water carrier: Wolsey's Palace was always short of water

All went well for Wolsey until 1525 when, finding himself very much out of favour, the house and its contents passed to the King. This event was graphically described in a despatch written by the Spanish Ambassador on 25 June 1525 in the following terms:

> When the King returned last from Windsor he passed by Hantoncourt [*sic*] a house belonging to the Legate, which he has presented to him with all its appurtenances, furniture etc. In future the Cardinal will lodge as any other of the King's servants.

The Spanish Ambassador may have been given to exaggeration, because Wolsey was still a power in the land when he received a huge French delegation at Hampton Court in 1527 for the discussions that were to lead to the signing of the Treaty of Hampton Court, but the final banquet was the last great occasion in which Wolsey took part there. He was visited by the French Ambassador in June 1528, although his influence was on the wane and his days at Hampton Court were numbered. In July and August 1528 he suffered a severe attack of the sweating sickness in the epidemic which lasted, around London, until the following January. By that time Henry VIII was using Hampton Court as his own house and Wolsey spent his last day at Hampton Court on 3 July 1529.

CHAPTER III

The Tudor Village and Green

Enormous though Wolsey's house was, it was not large enough for Henry VIII, so in 1529, some time before Wolsey's departure, he started to embellish and extend it greatly. In contrast to Wolsey's building, Henry VIII's building is very copiously documented in accounts preserved in the Public Record Office. Between April 1529 and August 1538 he built a new Kitchen and Buttery, and a Long Gallery consisting of new lodgings on the site of what we now know as the King's State Apartments. At the end of the Long Gallery was another gallery extending southwards to the river, where it ended in the Water Gate, which included the King's Baynes (baths) and the King's Library. New lodgings were built for the Queen, initially for Anne Boleyn but finished after her execution for Jane Seymour. Outside the Palace, in front of the Great Gatehouse and flanking the river, Henry built the Houses of Offices Without the Base Court and further away towards Hampton he built the King's New Stables.

The sheer magnitude of this addition to Wolsey's house can be gauged from the materials used – upwards of 25 million bricks, 1,275,000 tiles and more than 157 tonnes of lead, with proportionately huge supplies of stone and timber. Needless to say, the King wanted all this work completed 'with hastye expedicioun', and to achieve it he sent out

River traffic increased during the building of Henry VIII's Palace

over a large part of the country, from Norfolk, Suffolk, Essex and Kent in the east to Somerset, Gloucestershire and Herefordshire in the west, to recruit freemasons, bricklayers, carpenters and labourers. At any given time there would be as many as seventy-five carpenters, seventy-five bricklayers and 250 labourers working on the building, considerably more than in Wolsey's time. They were paid wages at a higher rate than they would get outside the Palace. As many of them came from far afield, accommodation for some of them had to be found in the villages on the far side of the river and the ferryman was kept busy from dawn to dusk. A string of small workshops for artisans such as smiths and carpenters sprang up just outside the boundary to Bushy Park from the north of Hampton Court Green to the gate into Bushy Park. Rough shacks were most likely attached to these for basic living accommodation. Many of the workmen, both skilled and unskilled, stayed on to found families. The village was increasing in size.

The accounts show that 'vetellyng howses' were set up on 'the Green', though these were not on The Green we know today, but near to the west front of the Palace. This land stretched from the Great Gatehouse on the west front of the Palace and fronted the river

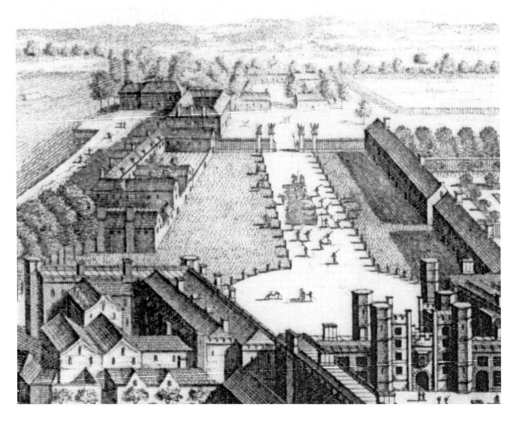

Victualling houses in the Outer Green Court. Extract from engraving by J. Kip, circa. 1702

until it narrowed at the point where the bridge to Taggs Island now stands. It included Hampton Court Green. In Tudor times it was as accessible to the world at large as the Royal Mews.

Occupying what is now the approach to Hampton Court Bridge, began the Timber Yard where the saw-pits and a wharf were situated. This is consistent with a number of entries in the accounts showing that the wharf of Henry VIII's time had been built on part of a small ait connected to the river bank by a causeway. This was just upstream of what is now the Middlesex end of Hampton Court Bridge in the immediate neighbourhood of the former Toy Inn; and it is reasonable to assume that the huge amounts of timber arriving at Hampton Court by river would be stored near to the wharf until required for use. Men were paid for 'keeping the timber yard in Crystenmasse time and all other stuff there'. It is interesting to find that the Christmas holidays in Tudor times lasted from about 21 December until 9 January. The Timber Yard merged with the Carpenters' Yard which flanked the highway from Hampton and can be identified as the area occupied by the houses now forming the southwest side of Hampton Court Green and some of the ground between them and the river.

A gate at the eastern up-river end of the Timber Yard led into the King's Meadow. The meadow was about 12 acres in extent and lay partly behind the Royal Mews. The rest of it ran westwards from the Royal Mews, between the highway and the river. The King's Meadow was used as a grazing area for cattle and sheep awaiting slaughter and must have been well used at times when the Court was in residence and as many as a hundred sheep would be slaughtered in a day.

In 1529 the victualling houses which were originally erected near to the Great Gatehouse in the part called Outer Green Court included a Great Bakehouse, a Privy Bakehouse, a Poultry Office and Scalding House (for the poultry), a Knife House and a Woodyard to store wood for fires. The houses were also known as Houses of Offices Without the Base Court. The occupants of the Palace must have been much relieved when the combined mix of noise, dust, smoke and pungent smells from the work in these buildings was moved outside the walls.

Part of the Timber Yard also served as a general storeyard at this time.

It was into this area that the supervisory officers were moved in 1536. The 'vetellyng howses' were also moved again in 1536 from their position 'beffor the King's gate' and re-erected in the Timber Yard. It appears fairly certain that their new position was where the Toy Inn later stood, the position marked by a plate set in the wall just to the right of the Trophy Gate entrance.

Between these buildings and the towpath was a branch of the moat. As there was already a moat round Wolsey's house, it seems likely that this was the

A bakehouse: sixteenth century

extension constructed in 1538 and described in the accounts as 'the mote by the Temmesyde'. A continuous supply of water from the Hampton spring came to these buildings and could have been used to flush waste to the moat and then to the Thames. Three bridges were built to connect the range of buildings to the towpath.

Again the local community benefited from the huge enterprise. This time the scope for employment included the parks and the King's new gardens. Women were paid two pence a day for weeding although Alice Brewer and Margaret Rogers received three pence a bushel for gathering primroses and violets for the gardens. Matthew Garrett was paid three pence a day for planting out the flowers which they had collected. The carpenters working on the high roof of the King's Great Hall were supplied with dozens of tallow candles by John Dowsett of Kingston. Bushels of wheat, oats and barley were purchased at Kingston market to feed the prized pheasants kept by the King.

For some centuries the western limit of the village of Hampton Court was the Hampton Gate at the end of Hampton Court Green. The Green itself is a piece of land which had at one time, before the Knights Hospitallers owned Hampton, been part of a long arable field running parallel to the Thames all the way from Hampton Court to Hampton itself.

At some time before Henry VIII became lord of the Manor of Hampton something over a quarter of a mile of the Hampton Court end of that field was enclosed as pasture land, perhaps for the Hospitallers' sheep or for Wolsey's animals; the horses, mules and other cattle necessary to a large household. It was already called The Green by 1534, when accounts for the mowing of bracken were recorded. The Green must have reached its present form some appreciable time after the land's use as arable had been abandoned, for its limits do not exactly correspond with the boundaries of the medieval field. There does not appear to be any ancient feature that forced the positioning of the Hampton Gate or the wall that separates The Green from the park.

The Hampton Gate at the end of The Green was necessary to stop animals which grazed on it from wandering on to the road leading to Hampton town. As the number of houses increased, The Green became a stinted pasture for the occupants' cattle and horses. A stint was the number of cattle which a holder of common rights was allowed to pasture on the commons. A gatekeeper was permanently stationed by it, with a little shed to keep him dry when he was not working.

As well as pasture, The Green was used for archery practice. There was plenty of room for target butts to be set up across it with space to spare for arrows that went astray or over-shot. It was still dangerous, though. On 14 July 1560 Thomas Tymperley was shooting at 'certain goals in the Great Park' when his arrow struck George Norton on the head and killed him. At the Coroner's inquest a few days later it was found that death had been caused by misadventure and Tymperley was pardoned. That incident may well have taken place on The Green, which was still officially part of the park.

The first mention of the Hampton Gate found in the Tudor records occurred in 1529, when John Van Guylders, the smith at the Wick, made a 'henge and a hooke for hampton gate waying xj li (5 kilograms)'. One reason ironwork of the time was so large and heavy was that the smiths were paid by the weight of metal used.

East View of the Gate on Hampton Court Green looking towards Hampton Court, Bernard Lens III, circa 1731-3. Yale Center for British Art, Paul Mellon Collection. The gate-keeper's hut is behind the fence on the right. See page 47 for the opposite view.

In 1531 the smith made 'a hoke for the parke gate towards h'mpton'. Although The Green was walled off from the rest of Bushy Park the gate at the end of it was still one of the named park gates, along with the Richmond Gate at Teddington and the Hanworth Gate, situated where the modern Duke's Head Passage in Hampton now is.

The 'greatt gate goyng to hampton' was mentioned in 1535, which means that by then there must have been a horse gate for men to open and ride through as well as a main gate which only needed to be opened, by the gatekeepers, when carts and carriages needed to pass.

There was a conduit head by the Hampton Gate in 1535, perhaps to water any traveller's horses, comparable to the horse-troughs which were so common until the middle of the last century. The Green continued as pasture for about three hundred years and by then the bracken on it was eventually mown out of existence.

The walls alongside the road from Hampton Court to Kingston were built by Thomas Clement in 1537-8. The black crosses outlined in black bricks in those walls were probably his trademark. Ernest Law noted their existence in the late nineteenth century although none remains today.

The intensive rebuilding programme at Hampton Court came to an abrupt end in August 1538 and no further accounts in detail exist for the Tudor period. The explanation of the sudden ending of these accounts comes to light in a paper in the *Letters and Papers, Foreign and Domestic* of Henry VIII. This paper records that a man named John Rede of Ewelme was charged with sedition in March 1539 and confined in Wallingford Castle. The nature of his alleged sedition, dating from some months back, was that he had spread a report that the King was dismissing all his workmen at Hampton Court and was going to build a new palace to be called Nonsuch. Another paper in the same series shows that there were good grounds for John Rede's report. On 16 November 1538 the Surveyor of Works, Comptroller of Works, Master Carpenter and Master Mason petitioned the Paymaster to make an end to payments at Hampton Court and to start paying at Nonsuch.

Several of the artisans at Hampton Court transferred to Nonsuch, near Epsom; John Van Guylders the smith worked there, Christopher Dickenson, a bricklayer at Hampton Court, became Master Mason, William Clement was employed as Master Carpenter and other craftsmen were also transferred to the new building site.

The only evidence of any work performed at Hampton Court between August 1538 and Henry VIII's death in 1547 is to be found in a few miscellaneous documents. These include records of the total amount expended in each year and of payments made to Nicholas Oursian for making the Great Clock in 1540. The Tiltyard must have been made at about this time, because the accounts for May 1537 record payment to the Master Carpenter and Master Bricklayer for going to other of the King's palaces to measure up the Tiltyards. There also is a report under the date 17 December 1542 of men working day and night to finish the lodgings of Katherine Parr, the sixth of Henry's Queens.

CHAPTER IV

Tudor Heirs

As the vast army of workmen moved to Nonsuch, there were periods of intense flurry and bustle when the Court was in residence at Hampton Court Palace. At those times the local community benefited from supplying the demands of a monarch with a retinue of about 2000 courtiers, statesmen and servants. A visit could last a few days or several months but after the state barges were rowed away and the dust of the creaking baggage wagons had settled as the Court moved on, the villagers would still have a part to play in the maintenance of the the Palace and its parks and gardens.

Henry VIII was succeeded by his three children in turn, firstly his son, Edward VI, who had been born in the Palace, but whose mother, Jane Seymour, succumbed about twelve days later. Edward VI was no more than nine years old when he came to the throne and it was his uncle, the Duke of Somerset, Protector of the Realm, who was the power behind the throne. Before long Somerset began to overplay his hand. Sensing that the Lords were endeavouring to curb his power, he issued a proclamation in the King's name calling all loyal subjects to assemble at Hampton Court and be ready to defend the King and himself. The towers were manned, the moat filled, and 500 suits of armour brought out of the armoury. The proclamation brought a large, but not very sympathetic crowd into the Outer Green Court before the Great Gatehouse, where they were addressed by the King and the Protector. Somerset's plan for rousing enthusiastic support failed and he left in some haste for Windsor Castle, taking the young King with him.

Edward VI died in 1553, before his sixteenth birthday, having spent a few brief periods during his reign in the Palace where he had been born, and without having made any changes affecting either the Palace or the village.

Edward's elder sister, Queen Mary, and her husband, Philip II of Spain, came to Hampton Court for their belated honeymoon in August 1554.

Mary was too forbidding and unattractive to command much love from her subjects, who also had little liking for the foreign king who had come amongst them. Mary was at Hampton Court again for her imagined pregnancy during the summer of 1555 and preparations were made there for the heralding of the birth that never took place. Like her young half-brother, she came and went without leaving a permanent memorial either in the Palace or in the village.

Elizabeth I had spent a fair amount of time at Hampton Court as a child, then for a time she was there as a prisoner of her half-sister, Queen Mary. It was at Hampton Court that, fortunately for England, the reconciliation took place thanks to the persuasive intervention of Philip. It was also at Hampton Court that Elizabeth was introduced to some of her suitors at secret meetings in the garden, and where she suffered an attack of smallpox in 1562 and another suspected attack in 1572. She continued to improve the gardens designed by her father and would spend her mornings walking in them. She is reported to have walked briskly when alone although she adopted a leisurely and regal manner in the presence of others in the gardens.

Elizabeth was at Hampton Court for a few short periods between her accession in 1558 and 1562, and then for longer periods for the Christmas and New Year festivities between 1568 and 1578. Her times spent at Hampton Court were occasions of much pomp and ceremony and she would entertain several hundreds of guests at Christmas with lavish feasts, masques, plays and dancing. These occasions gave employment to armies of carpenters who built and painted the stage and screens, to the merchants of silk and to the tailors who stitched it into sumptuous costumes as well as to the small team of workers who devised the lighting effects and on one occasion even caused artificial snow to fall.

There was then a long gap before the Queen came again for similar periods between 1592 and 1594.

The accounts for the reign of Elizabeth I show a period of general neglect, followed by hasty repairs when the Queen and Court were expected. As far as the village was concerned, the most important event was the building work to extend the Royal Mews. Henry VIII had demolished the Wolsey stables and rebuilt the 'Kyngs new stabyll' with a great stone gateway. In 1570 Elizabeth built two new barns and a coach house with garrets on to the western end of her father's stables which underwent extensive restoration at the

The stables of Henry VIII which were later extended by Elizabeth I

same time. These works took place at a time when she was beginning to stay at Hampton Court more frequently than she did during the early years of her reign. From 1579 to 1591 Elizabeth was never at Hampton Court.

Elizabeth's last visit to Hampton Court in 1599 was about three years before her death in 1603. The occasion was recorded by Lord Semphill, her Scottish Ambassador: '[The Queen's] visit to Hampton Court whence she went to Nonsuch. The day being passing foul, she *would* go on horseback although she is scarce able to sit upright.' The villagers who saw the bedraggled and windswept royal party set out little knew it was the last time they would see their Queen ride through the village.

CHAPTER V

The Stuart Village

There was a period of great industry in the Palace on the accession of James I, the new King from Scotland, in 1603. He very soon showed a partiality for Hampton Court and set in train a great programme of repairs and maintenance. Being short of money, he hit upon a novel source of revenue – the conferment of Honours. In Queen Elizabeth's time the conferment of knighthoods was a fairly rare event, but James I ordered that every owner of land worth £40 a year or more was required to receive a knighthood, for which a handsome fee was demanded. Failure to accept a knighthood in those days entailed a substantial fine.

The first Christmas of James I as King was celebrated at Hampton Court with much play-acting and merry-making. His Danish queen, Anne, enjoyed acting and joined in with the royal party who were involved in acting a specially commissioned masque. The young Inigo Jones designed the scenery. This was the occasion on which it seems very likely that Shakespeare himself acted in the Great Hall. Certainly the 'King's Men', of which company Shakespeare was a member, performed in several of the thirty plays which were staged during the festivities.

The following January Hampton Court was the scene of the great conference between the Church of England and the Puritans, the main result of which was the decision to produce a version of the Bible, the so-called King James Bible and referred to as the Authorised Version although strangely enough it never was authorised by Parliament.

The first year of James I's reign coincided almost exactly with the most disastrous visitation of the plague ever experienced in the Hampton area. The year before there had been in all eleven deaths, about the usual number, but during 1603 there were 119 deaths, of which ninety-nine were described as due to the plague. Of those who died a number were noted as

London citizens fleeing the plague. Hampton Court village also suffered outbreaks in plague years

having come from the Palace and some burials were recorded as having taken place in the King's Meadow.

During these early years, the village must have seen a great many new faces with the arrival of the would-be knights, of the players performing in the Christmas and New Year plays, and as if to provide an extreme contrast, the arrival of the godly, righteous and sober delegates to the Hampton Court Conference.

The ambitious programme of restoration and improvement within the Palace during the first years of James I's reign was not matched by a similar degree of activity outside. Almost the only work recorded in the accounts was the paving of a small yard at the Offices of Works, the erection of posts and rails in the Outer Green Court and at the Offices of Works to keep horses and coaches from the footway, and the new tiling of the roof of the Bakehouse after it had been damaged by fire in 1605.

By a strange chance the accession of Charles I coincided with another serious outbreak of the plague in the Hampton area, but this time it was by no means as devastating as the outbreak in 1603. Two of Queen Henrietta Maria's French priests caught it in the summer of 1625 and were kept in quarantine in a tower in the Tiltyard. In October of that year the King decided not to come to Hampton Court because of the plague at Windsor, but he did arrive for Christmas, when the number of those suffering in the area had fallen to six. There were further outbreaks later in his reign and in 1640 there were deaths among the grooms working in the King's Stable (the Royal Mews).

Like his mother, Charles I enjoyed the drama, and plays were given in the Great Hall. He also built up his great collection of pictures, and had a new organ installed in the Chapel. He had the 11-mile-long artificial river cut from Longford as an aid to the beautifying of the gardens with fountains and ponds. The Longford River, after crossing Bushy Park, goes underground just to the east of Glycine House, crosses under the road, and emerges to feed the canal in the Palace gardens.

During Charles I's reign the King's Stables were restored, the wharf and causeway were repaired, and some of the wooden pipes bringing water from the spring at Hampton to the Scalding House and the Bakehouse were re-laid.

The King's decision in 1639 to enclose a large area of land from Hampton Court to Richmond to make a deer park typified that lack of judgment which helped to lead to his downfall. Although he was persuaded to give up his plan, he was already set on the path which was to lead to the Civil War and his flight from the Palace in 1642. He was away from the Palace for five years and when he came back it was as a prisoner of the Roundheads. He arrived at Hampton Court on 24 August 1647 and on 11 November following he escaped with the help of some of his supporters and reached the Isle of Wight. For a time he was kept prisoner in Carisbrooke Castle, until he was brought back to London and tried for waging war against the Parliament and Kingdom of England, and condemned to death. Surprisingly, repairs were done to the Palace as need arose during the five years of the Civil War when the King was absent, as well as when he was there as a prisoner.

The Civil War did not end completely with the imprisonment of the King. There were Royalist uprisings in Kent and as close as Kingston in 1648. The village of Hampton Court was put in a state of alert and the ferryman was ordered to fix his boat to the Middlesex shore at sunset each day. Not many days passed, however, before the Royalists admitted defeat, and the village of Hampton Court had survived the Civil War without seeing any fighting; it all ended with the beheading of the King in front of his Palace of Whitehall on 30 January 1649.

A significant event in the history of the village occurred during Charles I's reign in 1636, when the Manor Court granted a piece of land close to the Palace to Nicholas Myles on copyhold tenure – the first piece of land to be so granted. Ivy House now stands on part of that land. Nicholas Myles, a thatcher by trade, was Under Keeper of the House (Home) Park at the time. Several members of the Myles family served the Crown at Hampton Court in various ways.

CHAPTER VI

Under the Protectorate

On 16 July 1649 Parliament, with Oliver Cromwell at its head, 'finding the office of a King in this nation to have been unnecessary, burthensome, and dangerous, hath utterly abolished the said Kingly office'. It had already been decided shortly before then to sell the late King's property to pay his debts and also to fill the coffers of the Commonwealth. Hampton Court was put up for sale with the other royal palaces. Most of the contents were sold, but no buyer was found for the Palace itself. After much indecision, the parks and the Stewardship of the Manor found buyers but shortly afterwards Cromwell was given the title of Lord Protector of the Commonwealth and the parks and the Stewardship were bought back again. Cromwell became the owner of the great estate that had belonged to kings and queens before him.

Parliament's determination at various times to dispose of the late King's property fortunately provided future historians with a very valuable source of information in the form of several surveys which were prepared for prospective purchasers. Of these the one made in 1653 is the most informative and it has been quoted extensively to describe the Palace and its appurtenances.

When Cromwell started to live in the Palace in 1654, he and his family must have led a frugal life there compared to that of Wolsey and the kings and queens. Most of the contents had been, or were still being, sold. Cromwell owned a substantial amount of furniture and carpets himself and together with the unsold tapestries and curtains he was able to entertain statesmen in a comfortable manner. All the time he was Protector, he was under threat of assassination and the Palace was closely guarded. It was said that, as a precaution, he would sleep in a different room each night and would vary his route to and from London each time he had to travel.

Cromwell continued the maintenance of the Palace and the ferryman, Simon Winsloo, was fully employed in ferrying over the workmen and labourers from the Molesey bank of the river. In 1656 he received a back payment of ten shillings for three months' work during the previous year.

It was in the Palace in 1658 that Cromwell suffered what was to prove his fatal illness. He was moved to London, and his condition grew worse. Shakespeare, if he had lived in a later age, would surely have relished the dramatic possibilities of the violence of the storm that broke on the eve of Cromwell's death, the most violent storm, it was said, for a hundred years past. The damage it caused at Hampton Court was still being repaired three years later. After his death a small body of servants was retained to guard the Palace and more were employed to look after and repair the water courses and the conduit pipes from Coombe and Hampton town.

Cromwell, when near his end, nominated his son Richard as his successor, but Richard Cromwell had none of the qualities required of a leader and did not command the respect of the nation as his nickname 'Tumble-down Dick' showed. Within a few months he withdrew from public life and the next step was taken by General Monk, one of Cromwell's most astute generals, who saw that the main hope for the stability of the country was to call Prince Charles back from exile. As a reward for his services Parliament passed a resolution offering General Monk the Palace of Hampton Court as well as its parks and perquisites. General Monk refused the Palace, but accepted the Stewardship of the Manor and the other offices that went with it, which left the Palace vacant for the Prince on his return to England at the end of May 1660. Before long General Monk was created Duke of Albemarle.

During Oliver Cromwell's tenure of the Lordship of the Manor a piece of land was granted by the Manor Court on copyhold tenure for the first time since Nicholas Myles's grant of 1636. This was to two widowed sisters, Mary Spurling and Mary Johnson, and the piece of land occupied approximately the site of the King's Arms public house, near to what was later to become the Lion Gate. This represented another step towards the development of the village of Hampton Court.

CHAPTER VII

Return of the Stuarts

The restoration of the monarchy brought a new lease of life to the Palace after the austerities of the Commonwealth period. One of the first things to be done was to test the loyalty of the Palace staff to the new King. It may well be that Cromwell's servants had already made themselves scarce, for the Lord Steward and his Board of Green Cloth found that only two, William Gunn, a Porter at the Gate, and Hugh Owen, a Child of the Scullery, were under suspicion, but were satisfied that 'they have now thoroughly purged and acquitted themselves'.

There was no shortage of loyal subjects who advanced claims for tangible recognition of their unswerving devotion to the Royalist cause during the Civil War. For some of them the reward was appointment to an office of profit under the Crown at Hampton Court, accompanied by a desirable lodging.

A period of restoration of the Palace buildings followed to make them fit not only for the new King, but also for his Queen, Catherine of Braganza, on her arrival at Hampton Court for their honeymoon on 29 May 1662; and, too, for the King's imperious mistress, Barbara Villiers, Countess of Castlemaine, later Duchess of Cleveland, who demanded full equality of status as far as apartments in the royal palaces were concerned.

Barely a month after the honeymooning couple had arrived, the first recorded road accident in Hampton Court took place. A groom of the Chapel Royal, Augustine Cleveland, was run over by a coach and horses on the roadway in front of the Great Gatehouse and was killed.

Improvements to the Tennis Court came in the first order of priority and in the House Park (now known as Home Park) the King had the great avenues of lime trees planted, many of them still growing sturdily. The only new building undertaken by Charles II was that of the apartments next to Paradise in the early 1670s. Paradise was the room at the south-east corner of the Palace where all the richest furnishings and tapestries were to be seen.

Activity in the Palace was reflected in a programme of work on the buildings outside. A new guard house was built at the entrance to the Outer Green Court, near to the site of the present Trophy Gates which implies that the previous open aspect of Outer Green Court was gated and fenced by that time. The Great and Privy Bakehouses, Scalding Office and Poultry Office were re-equipped with new ovens, dressers and shelves. Roofs were re-tiled, walls and ceilings re-plastered, and floors re-paved. The conduit which brought water from the Hampton spring had to be repaired 'when the water was lost and didn't come home'; and repairs were also carried out to the wharf and causeway.

The use of The Green as pasture had been in abeyance during Cromwell's tenure although soon after the Restoration it again was being used as a stinted pasture and William Bedborow, the Keeper of the King's Stables, was allowed to pasture four cows and one horse on The Green.

The Royal Mews was under the general jurisdiction of the Master of the Horse. Under him was the Surveyor or Keeper of His Majesty's Stables. William Bedborow had held the post since the time of Charles I and had maintained it under Cromwell. After the Restoration, however, it was reported that 'Wm Bedborow is a desperate and dangerous person, was an informer during the rebellion and is very unfit to serve the king' and he lost his entitlement to the office.

The influx of many extra people having employment in and about the Palace attracted a number of entrepreneurs who set up booths and tents in the Tiltyard for dispensing victuals. The Board of Green Cloth decided that this was happening too near to His Majesty's house, and could not be allowed, but a few were permitted to set up booths on The Green, including one, Patrick Lambe, who was allowed to have a monopoly for the sale of a supposed new luxury, tobacco.

The sale of tobacco was permitted on The Green

On the road to Hampton the houses and workshops forming the Offices of Works were given much attention. It appears that the new Surveyor-General of the King's Works, Sir John Denham, whose appointment was a reward for loyal service during the Civil War, saw to it that the highest priority was given to the Surveyor-General's own lodging. Improvements entailing a measure of rebuilding started in November 1660 and continued for upwards of three years. The wharf at the end of the Surveyor's garden was repaired and when Christopher Wren took over the post in 1670 a drawbridge from his garden to the wharf was set up.

Next in priority came the neighbouring lodgings assigned to the Master Carpenter, Master Mason, Master Locksmith, Paymaster, Comptroller of Works and Clerk of Works. The numerous workshops and storehouses in the Carpenters' Yard were also put in good order. The King's Stables nearby were repaired. The Timber Yard came into the news when the Board of Green Cloth ordered the Yeoman and Groom of the Flummery (desserts based mainly on oatmeal or flour) to collect every day the fragments from each table and carry them to the lodge at the gate of the Timber Yard and deliver them to the officers of the parish for the poor of Hampton and the Wick.

The granting by the Manor Court of pieces of land near the Palace on copyhold tenure continued and amongst those who received grants were:

Andrew Snape, Serjeant-Farrier to the Duke of Albemarle, a site near the ferry on which he built an inn later called the Mitre;

Abraham Fish, who planted the great avenues of lime trees, a site between the walls (Glycine House);

Thomas Mansfield, formerly a Major in the Duke of York's Regiment, which had been disbanded in 1679 (Park House).

The scandalous nature of the intrigues of Court life under Charles II must have supplied the village with endless snippets of gossip to enliven the tedium of long working days.

In January 1679 the eldest of Charles II's illegitimate sons, James Scott, Duke of Monmouth, as Commander-in-Chief of the Army issued an order for the men of the Duke of York's Regiment of Horse to assemble on The Green so that they could be paid off and the regiment disbanded.

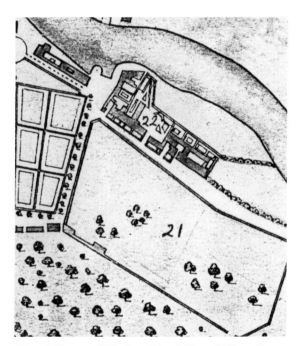

The younger brother of Charles II as Duke of York had lived on and off in his extensive apartments at Hampton Court. On coming to the throne as King James II in 1685 he made no attempt to conceal his determination to bring England back to Roman Catholicism, which before long set the country against him. The hatred he engendered by almost everything he did, and especially the reign of terror conducted by Judge Jeffreys in the Protestant West Country, sealed his fate and the country rejoiced in 1688 when he fled to the Continent and his son-in-law, the Prince of Orange, and his daughter, Princess Mary replaced him on the throne as King William III and Queen Mary II.

The Offices of Works (No. 22) and The Green (No. 21) with the ferry landing stage at the end of Frog Walk. Extract from map by C. Bridgeman, 1714

It is frequently said that James II spent no time at Hampton Court as King, but the records show that this was not so and that he did in fact spend a number of single days there in the summers of 1686 and 1687. The Palace and the buildings outside were by no means neglected during James II's reign. Repairs and maintenance continued normally, but there were no changes of any permanence.

CHAPTER VIII

The New Palace and the Village

The Prince of Orange landed at Torbay on 5 November 1688 and gathered support on his way to London. By Christmas James II had thrown his hand in, leaving Prince William with a clear field. Although he assumed power at once, it was not until the arrival of Princess Mary in February that Parliament invited them to reign jointly. The Princess was the nearer in the line of succession to the throne, but she refused to reign other than equally with her husband. King William and Queen Mary lost no time in going to see the Palace that had come into their possession at Hampton Court. Although there was much that pleased them about the situation, they found the Palace itself outmoded and inconvenient, and decided to make some drastic changes. One plan involved the demolition of almost the whole of the Tudor building and its replacement by an entirely new palace to the design of Sir Christopher Wren. In the event they demolished only the old State Apartments surrounding Cloister Green Court (the Fountain Court of the present day), Charles II's new building by Paradise, and the Water Gallery. The work started within a month of the decision being taken. Meanwhile Queen Mary used apartments in the Water Gallery down by the river and generally supervised the building operations. The work started at a goodly pace, but before long she became impatient at the slow progress, which was attributable partly to lack of money, but also to the blockade of the Channel by the French fleet impeding the supply of Portland stone.

William and Mary, in their determination to create the greatest royal palace in Europe, wanted everything ship shape in the Royal Mews. A large programme of structural repairs was begun and the hay barn was converted into another stable and a Dutch barn was erected to the west of the Mews for storing hay.

It was hardly surprising that when William and Mary started making such profound changes at Hampton Court one of the first things to happen was the digging of foundations for new guard houses, one for the Foot Guards which was nearer to the entrance to the Outer Green Court and the other, nearer to the Great Gatehouse, for the Horse Guards. Four tall gate piers were erected where Trophy Gate now stands.

An important activity on the Green at the time of the rebuilding of the Palace was the digging of gravel, and some large pits were dug towards the north-east side of The Green. These pits provided gravel for the walks in the garden and for surfacing the roads. In due course these pits were filled up with rubble from the demolition of the old state apartments and other buildings, but one of the pits remained and can be seen as a small sunken garden and lake in the grounds of Hampton Court House.

The victualling houses of Henry VIII's time had their parallel in 1689 during these building works. Again the great influx of building craftsmen of all sorts had to be accommodated and The Green was the nearest available piece of common land. It was the appearance of their sheds, workshops and refreshment places that precipitated a survey of encroachments by the Manor Court. Apart from the buildings which bordered The Green and developed into permanent structures there were at least ten temporary buildings scattered on it, mostly 18 to 50 feet (5.5 to 15.2 metres) wide and anything up to 72 feet (21.9 metres) long. The survey of encroachments gives the names of the owners of these sheds and the occupations of several of them have been traced.

A blacksmith's forge

Andrew Snape, landlord of the Mitre and the King's Serjeant-Farrier, had a forge in one of the sheds and William Bache who was Master Locksmith for nearly twenty years from 1680 had his forge there. As Master Locksmith he was responsible for making all the locks, keys, latches and hinges required. He was succeeded as Master Locksmith by Josiah Key who continued to use the forge on The Green and whose delicately designed and perfectly made brass door locks can still be seen on Palace doors. He was so advanced in his ideas as to make rising joint hinges.

Some of the temporary sheds had been pulled down before the end of 1691 but in 1700-1 some more were erected to replace buildings, which, with the virtual completion of the King's State Apartments, had been removed from the nearby gardens. The great Jean Tijou, the French smith who designed all the decorative ironwork in the new Palace as well as the magnificent panels or screens at the end of the Privy Garden, executed much of it himself. He had a new forge set up on The Green in 1701 to complete this work. William Bushell, who was a general carrier and contractor, had a shed there where he kept all his wheelbarrows and 'drugs' (timber trucks).

Stephen South was a wheelwright and in his shop on The Green he made wheelbarrows and drugs, sledgehammer and pickaxe handles as well as carrying out repairs and maintenance. Thomas Church was a paviour who also had a shed. He was called on to lay all the new paving in the Palace including the courtyards and the yard at the Royal Mews. John Webb had a carpenter's shop and Nathaniel Winch, who was a brewer and distiller, had a house of refreshment. Charles Browne, the accountant for the building who worked for three years from 1689, also had a shed on The Green where he kept his books.

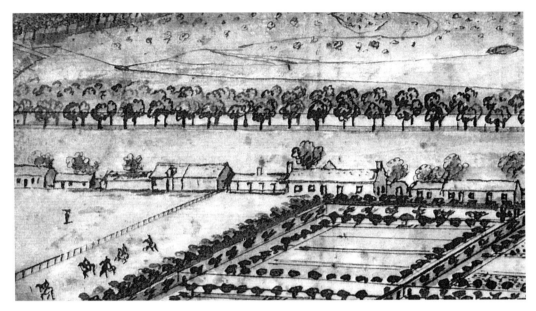

Workshops on The Green. Robert Stephenson's refreshment house and Clarence Place are also shown. Extract from preparatory drawing by L. Knyff for *Bird's-eye View of Hampton Court'*, 1702. © The British Museum

Although in 1690 a committee of copyholders was set up 'to view and tak an acct. of the several buildings that have been lately erected at Hampton Court and between the walls of the Parke and upon the Wast, and to informe the Court who the several persons are who have built and erected the same', the Manor Court took no immediate steps to have them removed. Some of the sheds were taken away in 1691 but as much as eight years later Jasper English, Under Housekeeper of the Palace and proprietor of the Toy Inn, reported that 'sheds having become cottages will prove prejudicial to H.M. Palace if not removed', and in the course of time they were either removed or rebuilt in permanent fashion with the approval of the Manor Court. Widow Lawrence disregarded instructions to demolish her small cottage against the park wall in 1691 but was finally forced to pull it down in 1701 and rebuild it in another place.

In 1690 the old building which had served as the Offices of Works headquarters, including the lodgings of the Comptroller, Clerk and Paymaster of the Works, was pulled down and a new one put up. In a survey of encroachments in the same year there was reference to 'one shed on the backside of the Woodhouse neare the Thames in the occupation of Timothy Amedee, in length 27 foot in breadth 11 foot for the Kings Doggs'. Where the King's dogs were kept before that time is not known but there was quite a large dog population in the neighbourhood to cater for the hunting and coursing which had long been the sports of kings and queens. Shortly after the survey this was pulled down and a new dog kennel was built on the far side of Kingston.

Immediately the plan to rebuild the Palace became known, Robert Stephenson, the landlord of the Toy Inn, evidently with an eye to the main chance, managed somehow to take over the Mitre Inn. This did not at all suit the book of the Board of Green Cloth, who were quick to note that Robert Stephenson 'monopolizeth all ye trade of such Gentlemen and others as resort to his Ma'ties Court' and ordered him to hand over the Toy to Jasper English, the Under Housekeeper of the Palace, whose perquisite it was. Mr Stephenson then put up a refreshment house at the corner of The Green near to where Craven House now stands. Whether he gave up the Mitre as well as the Toy is not known, but a few years later, in 1696, he was granted the copyhold tenure of the land on which his new refreshment house stood.

The oldest shops in the village were those belonging to Jasper English, Under Housekeeper to the Palace. In 1693 he was granted a piece of land lying between the Mitre and adjoining his official residence as Under Housekeeper, Palace Gate House which is now the site of two houses known as Palace Gate House and The Green. On this piece of land he built three shops – a barber's, a suttler's and a butcher's at Nos 1, 2 and 3 Palace Gate. The suttler's did a roaring trade selling provisions and beer to the large number of soldiers now living in the new Guard Houses. Plans show the immediate surroundings of the butcher's shop included beast pens, piggeries and a slaughterhouse. It seems likely that the slaughterhouse was in response to a demand from the Board of Green Cloth which, in 1689, had complained of the lack of such a facility near the palace and the need to hire one at Kingston.

In May 1690 Sir Christopher Wren wrote to the Board of Green Cloth that many booths had been set up near to the Palace for the sale of ale and other liquors and that this brought 'many vicious and idle people' to the neighbourhood 'to pilfer and steal the materials prepared for their Ma'ties buildings'. The Board at once ordered all such booths to be demolished and no new ones to be set up without a licence.

This reign saw an increase in the number of grants of land under copyhold tenure. Apart from Robert Stephenson's grant noted above, grants were made to:

Widow Lawrence, widow of William Lawrence, a site on the road to Kingston (where No. 1 Clarence Place, Clarence Cottage and Norfolk Cottage now stand)
William Thatcher, blacksmith, a site 'Between the Walls' (now Clarence Lodge)
Christopher Garraway, the King's smith, a house that used to be on a site just east of the Flower Pot Gate on the south side of the road
Henry Peacock, Keeper of the Balcony Garden, a site 'Between the Walls' (now Lancaster Lodge and York Lodge).

There were also encroachments by Lord Portland and Lord Lumley, noted by the Manor Court in the survey of encroachments in 1690, but not registered as copyhold tenures until many years later.

The sudden death of Queen Mary from smallpox in 1694 at the early age of thirty-two was a catastrophe for King William and he had no heart for carrying on with the building. So for the next three to four years scarcely anything was done to the new Palace. Then, in

January 1698, the Palace of Whitehall was almost completely destroyed by fire, and to make up for this loss the King decided to continue with the new building at Hampton Court. By the end of 1699 it was sufficiently near to completion for him to move in, and he lived there periodically until his death in March 1702. During his last years, the great avenue of lime and chestnut trees was planted in Bushy Park. This avenue had been designed by Sir Christopher Wren as a magnificent approach to his planned entrance to a rebuilt palace which was to be in a line from a new gateway, the huge Lion Gate. Although Wren's plans were never completed, the avenue flourished and a new gateway into Bushy Park was made in the park wall. Previously, entrance had been through a gate known as Harewarren Gate, which was almost opposite Flowerpot Gate. This eventually fell into disuse and has now disappeared under later buildings.

The greater part of the building of the new Palace and the decoration of the King's State Apartments had been completed by the end of William III's reign. From then onwards it was mainly a question of finishing touches. Queen Anne rarely used Hampton Court as a residence, though she sometimes came over from Windsor to hold meetings of the Privy Council. At the end of 1710 she seems to have had the intention of coming more frequently, for it was then that she ordered the levelling and preparation of ground in both the House Park and Bushy Park to make chaise rides, which would enable her to drive a chaise to and fro for a distance of about twenty miles. She did occasionally make use of the chaise rides and Jonathan Swift recorded in his journal the Queen 'drives furiously, like Jehu'.

Her visits up to her death were few and far between. When the Palace was being prepared for Queen Anne's first visit in 1706, rules were drawn up for the staff of the Scalding House in the following terms:

> to receive from Poulterers no more Fowll than will be spent in one day's service
> not to pressure delivery of any kind of provision but what is directed by the
> Clerk of the Kitchen
> not to receive any grown rabbits into the Office after Xmas Day
> not to be allowed more than one pullet to as many giblets as are necessary to
> make a Pye
> not to take any fee other than rabbit skins, feathers and giblets of fowl.

After about 1700 the demand for building craftsmen diminished. This meant that the Master Carpenter, Master Mason, Master Bricklayer and Master Plasterer were not often required to be at Hampton Court, but were engaged on work at other palaces. The Master Gardener, on the other hand, was still a leading light and there were many alterations and improvements to the gardens and parks during Queen Anne's reign.

In 1706 Sir Christopher Wren, then a man of seventy-four, first applied for permission to rebuild his official house to make a home for himself during his declining years, observing that the Crown did owe him £341 3s 4d and that he would be prepared to forgo this amount, if his wish were granted, which it eventually was on 19 June 1708. This was to be an important stage in the history of the village – the rebuilding of the houses originally built for the principal Officers of Works in Henry VIII's time, to make them much as we still see them today.

Very early in Queen Anne's reign a new luminary appeared on the scene at Hampton Court. The Comptroller of the Works, William Talman, retired in the summer of 1702 and was succeeded by the architect and playwright, Sir John Vanbrugh. Vanbrugh was therefore entitled to the use of the Comptroller's lodging, but he chose not to move there. Before the end of Queen Anne's reign he was manipulated out of office, but was restored to it soon after the accession of George I.

In 1704 the Royal Gardener, Henry Wise, was granted a plot against the middle part of the wall of Bushy Park on the north-east side of Hampton Court Road and almost opposite to his official house, the Master Gardener's House which later became known as Wilderness House. With this grant and those of previous reigns a great deal of the available land lying between the east corner of The Green and Hampton Wick had been disposed of and houses were built on a number of the plots. Seven brick houses with tiled roofs had been erected on plots along the northeast part of Hampton Court Road with adjacent coach houses and stables as well as two

Henry Wise, Master Gardener

inns and a refreshment house. Workshops on The Green also had living accommodation and on the south side of The Green the substantial houses of the Offices of Works ran down to the river. By now, the Toy and the Mitre were well established inns and the shops at Palace Gate were thriving. The village was beginning to take the shape it is today.

CHAPTER IX

Hanoverian Influence

On the death of Queen Anne there was no Protestant heir to the throne in the direct Stuart line, and it fell to George, the Elector of Hanover, great-grandson of James I through his daughter Elizabeth of Bohemia, to become King. He had condemned his wife, Sophia Dorothea, to a life in prison, because of her love affair with Count Koenigsmarck. There was therefore no Queen to reign with King George I. Instead, he brought with him his two friends, Frau Kielmansegge (who was also his half-sister) and Frau Schulenberg, who were familiarly known as the 'Maypole' and the 'Elephant and Castle'. Later they were ennobled as Countess of Darlington and Duchess of Kendal respectively; both were intensely disliked by the populace.

Only one copyhold grant was made by the Manor Court in George I's reign and that was for another plot of land 'Between the Walls' in 1714. The recipient, John Huggins, had no part in the building or maintenance of the Palace, gardens or parks, but held an office under the Crown as Keeper of Westminster Palace. He was also Warden of the Fleet Prison, the debtors' prison which gained such evil repute.

On the south side of Hampton Court Road, running eastwards from the Flowerpot Gate entrance to the Palace, is a triangular glade overshadowed by trees and mottled in spring with daffodils. This plot is much smaller than it was before the road was widened in 1900 and it is difficult now to picture it as the site of a house with several outhouses and a yard and garden. The Longford River passes through a culvert under this glade to feed the Canal and the Long Water. In earlier times the river was open here and was crossed by a wooden bridge which appears to have been in need of substantial repairs about every three years. Part of this plot, on which a forge used by William Lawrence had already been erected, was granted to Christopher Garraway in 1692. He disposed of it to Robert Burford, a Palace carpenter who built a small house.

John Huggins purchased this house in 1714 and persuaded the Manor Court to grant him an extra plot of land, the part under which the Longford River flows. He also obtained the use of a plot against the park wall on the opposite side of the road for his coach house and stables. John Huggins, in common with other Wardens of the Fleet Prison, grew rich on the proceeds of bribery but in 1729 he was on trial at the Old Bailey on a charge of murdering a prisoner by confining him in a strong room which was over an open sewer, had no form of bedding or heating and was used as a mortuary. He was discharged on the grounds that it could not be proved that he knew that the conditions in the strong room were detrimental to life. After his disgrace, the house and land were sold.

In 1718 posts and rails along Hampton Court Green were carried to 'the gate leading to

Hampton Town so as the Green may be preserved and kept in good order thereby'. A map of about 1735 shows the gate as one large central single-hinged swinger with gaps on each side.

During the reigns of George I and George II, The Green was often used as a camp for the military. The First Regiment of Guards was encamped there in 1716 and George II

An East View of the Quarter Guard on Hampton Court Green, Bernard Lens III, 1733. Yale Center for British Art, Paul Mellon Collection

gave orders in 1728 for a battalion of Guards to be encamped on The Green and to provide the guard whenever he was in residence at the Palace.

The last stages in the rebuilding of the Palace took place during the first eight years of George II. The buildings remaining from the Tudor period on the east side of the Inner Court were reported to be unsafe, and this resulted in their being rebuilt in 1732 to form apartments for William, Duke of Cumberland, the King's second surviving son, who was to become such an object of hatred for his part in suppressing the 1745 uprising in Scotland led by the Young Pretender.

The lamb pen belonging to the butcher's shop at Palace Gate figured in the accounts of Hampton's Overseers of the Poor in 1737, vividly portraying the hard life of the poor at that time:

Bote for the Woman that was Brought to Bed in Sigin's Lam Pen, the midwife and Nurse and keepin in the time of her Lyin Inn & Bering her Child and Getting Her a Way . . . £2 3s 2d

In 1735 the Queen's Great Staircase was eventually completed with the painting of the walls and ceiling. Only two years later George II's Queen, Caroline, died and with her death the Palace virtually came to an end as a royal residence. The King made occasional visits after that time, but generally only for the day. This resulted in the lack of care given to the Palace. In 1742 the Clerk of Works reported that rain was coming through the roof. From then on he was constantly being reminded that he was to do no more in the way of repairs than was absolutely necessary to keep out the wind and rain; that expenditure must be kept to a minimum; and that old materials were to be used as far as possible.

A change in the relationship between the Palace and the village was now becoming evident. The copyhold leases which had been granted to officials of the Crown or of the Government were changing hands by inheritance, but the new generations did not usually succeed to the offices of their fathers. The sale of copyhold leases likewise brought in new owners who held no official position. Even the houses still belonging to the Crown were beginning to be occupied by such people. Wren's house had passed to his son Christopher, whose office of Deputy Clerk Engrosser had become a sinecure many years before. He had become a Member of Parliament in 1712, and it then passed to Sir Christopher's grandson, Stephen who had no connection with the Palace.

Several new copyhold tenures were granted during George II's reign. Sir Robert Walpole, the first Prime Minister, was granted a plot of land 208 feet by 25 feet (63.4 by

The first Hampton Court bridge, 1753. The Mitre and the Toy Inn face each other on the far bank

7.6 metres) in 1731 on which he built a house, a coach house and stables. This was next to the new entrance to Bushy Park and opposite Wilderness House. Lord Scarborough (formerly Lord Lumley) and Lord Portland were granted the plots on which they had encroached many years before. The Lion Gate Hotel occupies one of these plots today. George Lowe, one of Henry Wise's successors as Royal Gardener, was granted in 1743 the plot on the north-east side of The Green where Prestbury House now stands. Lastly, in 1757 George Montagu Dunk, Earl of Halifax, built himself the large house known as Hampton Court House, though the formal granting of the lease did not take place until four years later.

The first Hampton Court Bridge was open to the public in 1753 after persistent demand for easier transport from residents on both the Middlesex and Surrey banks of the river. Permission for building of the bridge gained the royal assent after strong lobbying by James Clarke who was lessee of the Manor of East Molesey as well as of the Hampton Court ferry. The ferry had been leased to the Clarke family for about a century. A curious structure, reminiscent of a Chinese bridge, it proved unequal to the task and was replaced after twenty-five years.

CHAPTER X

Changing Times

A new era started for Hampton Court Palace and Village when George III resolved never to live there. However, appreciating that the Palace would suffer from want of occupation, he decided to grant suites of apartments, by grace and favour of himself, to persons who had distinguished themselves in the service of their country or of the Crown. More often than not it came about that the apartments were granted to the next of kin. Not long after the introduction of the 'grace and favour' concept, about 1775, the Houses of Offices in Outer Green Court – the Great and Privy Bakehouses, Poultry Office, Scalding Office and the Woodyard Office, by then usually known as the Trophy Gate Buildings – were converted into residences.

The royal grooms were in attendance at the Royal Mews on the occasions when Queen Anne, George I and George II were in residence, but now there was no call for them to be there. Some of the 'grace and favour' residents in the palace were allowed the use of the coach houses and stables in the Mews, including living accommodation for their grooms.

At the beginning of George III's reign the King's Meadow was let and the income from it became a perquisite of the Housekeeper of the Palace, Mrs Elizabeth Mostyn. In 1785, after the death of Mrs Mostyn, the copyhold of a plot of land adjoining the Royal Mews was granted to Mrs Spilsbury. She had been Mrs Mostyn's faithful companion and was her sole executrix who sold it two years later to David Feltham, the prosperous toll-keeper of Hampton Court Bridge. Before long he built a house there which later became the Cardinal Wolsey public house. The new building was between the western end of the Royal Mews and a small house built on land granted to Thomas Davis, the village butcher, in 1772. This was to become a beer shop called the Henry VIII in 1841, the year when the Cardinal Wolsey opened as a public house.

The house which had once been owned by John Huggins to the east of Flowerpot Gate was demolished in 1787 and the copyhold of the site was sold back to the Crown which resulted in this plot remaining the open space it is today.

At the end of the eighteenth century the Palace had a near-royal occupant when Prince William of Orange, the Stadtholder of the Netherlands, stayed there as George III's guest, after fleeing from the French invasion of his country. Prince William was the King's cousin, being the son of George II's eldest daughter Anne. The Prince brought his family and a large retinue with him and they must have had an especially warm welcome from the tradespeople of Hampton Court who supplied their wants from 1795 until 1802, when they returned to their homeland after the Treaty of Amiens.

As part of an economy drive in 1782 the office of Under Housekeeper was abolished (though the holder of that office was able to enjoy an adequate pension for another thirty-five

The second Hampton Court Bridge which was completed in 1778

years) and the salary of the Housekeeper was reduced. By that time it was possible for visits to be made to the State Apartments by arrangement with the Housekeeper (usually a titled lady or not far removed from a title), who was allowed to pocket the expected gratuity. Some visitors complained that they were hurried around so quickly by one of the Housekeeper's underlings that they had no time to look properly at the pictures. Presumably the Housekeeper was only too anxious to have the tour completed as quickly as possible so that another one could start and she could increase her income.

Another result of the 1782 economies was a recommendation by the Treasury that the houses on the south-west side of The Green should be sold outright – the houses originally constituting the Office of Works, where the principal officers had also resided. Action on this recommendation was dilatory and in the end it was reversed by an Act of Parliament with the result that these houses remained Crown property until the freeholds began to be purchased by residents from the 1970s onwards.

The policy established during the previous reign of doing only sufficient repairs to the Palace to keep out the wind and rain and to keep the building from falling down was continued in George III's reign. But in 1771 a major piece of reconstruction was forced upon the Board of Works when the Great Gatehouse was seen to be in danger of collapse. This was not the first time that it had been found to be in a precarious state and as far back as Charles II's time the front of it had needed to be shored up. In 1771 the Board of Works, which then included William Chambers and John Adam, decided that it must be rebuilt quickly. The original five storeys were reduced to three and parts of the Gatehouse were faced with a red brick, which was in unfortunate contrast with the colour of the Tudor brick, and to this day shows up as a stain on the west front of the Palace.

An important change which was to affect the area for many years to come was George III's decision in 1794 to allow the posting of a Troop of Cavalry to Hampton Court. This incurred the taking over of the King's Chaise Marine House which stood on The Green against the Bushy Park wall between the gravel pit and the site on which Prestbury House now stands. This had been built in 1733 for the shelter of the King's two large carriages of a type known as a chaise marine. It was now converted into barracks which were to remain until 1811 when a new barrack block was built on the site which is now a coach and car park on The Green. The land on which it had stood was absorbed into that of Hampton Court House. The Royal Mews was adapted for the accommodation of men and horses of the Horse Artillery. The Keeper of the Mews had a windfall when he was allowed to supplement his income by converting the eastern part of his lodging into an inn. This was known by the sign of the Chequers.

In 1812 the Manor Court consented to forgo all right or claim to Hampton Court Green as waste land and all right of pasturage on it. This was on condition that the King gave up a claim for common land in Hampton. It was also agreed that no part of The Green should be built on and that the fence enclosing it should be no more than four feet high. Today The Green is the responsibility of Historic Royal Palaces.

As the importance of the Palace declined there came an increase in the importance of the gardens for the production of fruit out of season and other delicacies for Windsor Castle. From Henry VIII's time the gardens had been producing large crops of fruit, and Henry Wise had planted a wide variety of fruit trees – 181 peaches and nectarines, 155 cherries, 110 pears, 144 plums, 49 figs, 60 apples, 26 apricots and 12 quinces; and melons were a regular crop. While the greatest economies were being enforced as far as the fabric of the building was concerned in the latter half of the century, substantial sums could be found for the cultivation of early fruit, including pineapples, grapes, oranges and strawberries; and of mushrooms and asparagus.

The Master Gardener during part of this period (1765–1783) was the renowned Lancelot ('Capability') Brown. It was during his time in the post that the Great Vine was planted in the Palace grounds. He was designing gardens over a large area of the country, so can have spent only a small part of his time at Wilderness House, his official house at Hampton Court. Indeed he seems to have neglected his duties as Royal Gardener, for in 1770 he was reprimanded by the Board of Works for leaving undone the things which he ought to have done in the gardens. It may be that he lost interest in the gardens when he found that there was little opportunity for imposing his ideas on their established design.

Apart from Lancelot Brown, there were several other well-known residents in the village in George III's reign, including William Chambers, usually known as Sir William, though his knighthood was a Swedish one. As Comptroller of the Board of Works he had an official house in the Office of Works, but was edged out of it during the economy drive of 1782. Other distinguished officers of the Board of Works who lived in Hampton Court Village from time to time included Thomas Ripley and Henry Flitcroft (Vanbrugh's successors as Comptroller). Across The Green at Hampton Court House lived the mistress of the Earl of Halifax, then the Earl of Suffolk, and after him the Earl of Sandwich (inventor of the sandwich).

A West Prospect of the Gate on Hampton Court Green to Hampton Town, Bernard Lens III, circa 1731-3. Yale Center for British Art, Paul Mellon Collection. The gatekeeper's hut is on the left.

The Hampton Gate was finally abandoned about 1810. Henry Ripley, writing in 1884, records:

> At this spot [at the far western end of The Green], within the last eighty years, existed a gate, stretched completely across the road, and attended to by an ancient party who inhabited a sort of watch box at the extremity nearest the river. The purport of this institution – 'Bob's Gate' as it was called – was to prevent cattle from straying within the precincts of the village, and helping themselves to the succulent cabbage or nutritious turnip gracing the gardens of the frugal villagers.

By Ripley's time, though, The Green was no longer pasture ground but merely a pleasant stretch of grass on which fairs and festivals were occasionally held.

CHAPTER XI

From Villager to King

On 26 June 1830 the Duke of Clarence was aroused from his sleep at Bushy House to hear that his brother, King George IV, had died and that he had succeeded to the throne. He is said to have replied in characteristic fashion that he did not intend to get up straight away as he had never before been in bed with a queen. Regarding themselves as fellow parishioners of the new King, the residents of Hampton Court Village joined with those of Hampton in submitting a special address of loyalty to him and the Queen.

As Duke of Clarence, the new King had many friends in the village. During his time at Bushy House he had lived the life of a gentleman farmer. He played a full part in the local community and was a member of the vestry of St Mary's church in Hampton and had entered his name in the ranks of the local 'Volunteers of Infantry and Cavalry'. His was a familiar face at local sporting events of cricket and boxing. The Toy Inn was a favourite place to meet his friends for an evening of drinking and cards.

The Toy Inn had been rebuilt at the end of the seventeenth century together with a line of stables and coach houses parallel to the river behind the tap room of the Toy. Altogether, around thirty horses could be stabled in this range of buildings. Mail coaches would stop for a change of horses and to deliver and collect letters and packages. A small building with a bay window to the left of Trophy Gate served as a Post Office for the collection of mail.

The Toy was doubtless best known for the Toy Club, whose members were drawn from the gentry living around Hampton Court. Its main activity was to meet once a month for dinner, local gossip, the singing of seafaring and drinking songs and much rowdy jollification. It had many distinguished members of which the Duke of Clarence was one. Marrow pudding was the speciality which was served when he was present. The Toy was a favourite meeting place for sports enthusiasts after the horse racing, the prize fighting or the cricket on Molesey Hurst. The Duke of Clarence long remembered his convivial evenings at the Toy and when he became King he granted a 'grace and favour' apartment in the Palace to the daughter of William Smart, the innkeeper.

The structure of the Toy was never very sound. It is possible that the foundations had been undermined by

A pewter tankard engraved 'Toy Inn Hampton Court', early nineteenth century. The collection of John Sheaf

The Toy Inn (right) as seen from the Molesey bank in the eighteenth century with the Mitre (left). The second bridge at Hampton Court was a wooden eleven-span structure. It survived until 1865. Thomas Rowlandson. By permission of the V & A Picture Library

flooding. In 1829 the entrance hall was flooded to a depth of nearly a metre and boats were taken through it. In 1830, the year that one of its best customers became the King of England, it shut its doors for the last time and on 9 September five years later a memo from the Treasury sealed its fate: 'The Lords of His Majesty's Treasury have been pleased to sanction the selling by Public Auction the Material of the Old Toy Inn at Hampton Court to be taken down and cleared away.' By 1840 all traces of the inn had vanished.

After ascending the throne, William IV and Queen Adelaide could not take as much part in local life as they had previously, but the King took out an insurance policy for Queen Adelaide, his junior by twenty-seven years, by having her created Ranger of Bushy Park and Chief Steward of the Honor and Manor of Hampton Court. As she was still regarded as a fellow parishioner by the inhabitants of Hampton Court Village, her birthday used to be celebrated with much merry-making on The Green.

In 1832 the village butcher at Palace Gate was James Turner. His neighbour who lived at Palace Gate House, which was once part of the house belonging to the Under House-keeper, was Dr Baker, the village doctor. Dr Baker complained to the Office of Woods, Forests and Public Buildings about the state of Mr Turner's yard. The Office's surveyors recommended that the slaughtering of animals on Mr Turner's premises should be prohibited. Mr Turner refused to accept this as a condition of his tenure and he was given notice to quit four years later. By that time Dr Baker had moved to The Green next door which had been divided from Palace Gate House in 1734. This continued to be the home of the village doctors until the outbreak of the Second World War.

By now Hampton Court was becoming more like a traditional English village. True, the inhabitants were still to some extent dependent on the bounty of the great house, though that bounty was more diffuse than before. Visitors were coming from far afield to look at the Palace and perhaps be taken on a tour by the Housekeeper and crowds were flocking to Bushy Park and also to Molesey Hurst just across the river for the cricket, horse-racing and prize-fighting, all patronised by royalty and nobility at various times; there were also the troops.

All of this was good for trade and a wide range of businesses came into being. There was a grocer at No. 3 Palace Gate, a baker still working in the Bakehouse in Outer Green Court and a caterer, saddler, fruiterer and a butcher's shop on the north-east side of Hampton Court Road. A few enterprising folk set up stalls at the Palace gates, but were soon banished by the Board of Works. There was not much movement of population into and out of Hampton Court Village and some traders continued for three generations, such as Robert Evans, the grocer. There were also many families who could boast that they 'were not connected with trade', who remained in the village. So it came about that in the first half of the nineteenth century a number of family names became especially associated with Hampton Court,

Advertisement for a hair-cutter and dresser to the 'Nobility, Gentry and Public of Hampton Court', 1822

the Felthams, Hetheringtons, Lapidges, Newberys, Ives and Hippersons.

By 1837 the list of inhabitants included some more well-known names. Admiral Lord Keith lived at Hampton Court House for a few years. As Captain Elphinstone he had been the Duke of Clarence's commanding officer, and in 1815 it was he who was entrusted with the removal of Napoleon to St Helena. Another nobleman, the 3rd Earl of Kerry, lived there from 1816 to 1818. Admiral Bowater lived at what was later known as Bowater House, now Craven House.

On 5 April 1832 there was a governmental reorganisation. The Office of Works was amalgamated with the Office of Woods and Forests. At Hampton Court the effects of this change were the downgrading of the post of Labourer in Trust, held by Mr George Slade, as Clerk of the Works, and the allocation of the overall supervision of the Palace to Mr Edward Jesse, Surveyor of Woods, Forests, Parks and Buildings.

CHAPTER XII

Visitors Meet the Village

Very soon after her accession Queen Victoria decided that she would not use Hampton Court Palace as a residence, and took the bold step of opening the State Apartments to the public, free, on every day of the week except Friday, when it was to be closed for cleaning. The time was made opportune by the death of Lady Emily Montague in April 1838. She was the last to hold the office of Lady Housekeeper and to be entitled to the fees for allowing visitors to see the Palace. Action was not long delayed and a letter bearing the date 17 August 1838 was sent by their Lordships at the Treasury to Mr Jesse informing him that the arrangements he had proposed for the admission of the public to the State Apartments had been sanctioned. The public at large was very quick to take advantage of the opportunity to see the inside of the Palace. In the first year of opening 115,971 visitors were counted, and it used to be said that on summer Sunday afternoons in the 1840s people were passing through at the rate of more than a thousand an hour. In the year of the Great Exhibition, 1851, the number of visitors soared to 350,848.

The opening of the State Apartments inevitably brought about further changes in the village. The number of refreshment houses grew considerably. No. 2 Palace Gate was united with No. 1 and both were occupied by the Palace police together with Palace Gate House. After the police moved out in 1858, No. 1 became the village Post Office which had previously opened in a small building on the north side of Trophy Gate where a telephone box now stands. The first pillar box had been erected three years earlier to deal with the increased volume of mail after the Penny Post had been introduced in 1840 and the one standing in Palace Gate today is on the site of the original pillar box for the village. When the Post Office moved away, No. 1 became a confectioner's. In 1850 an infants school was started in a corner of the Bakehouse in the Outer Green Court for children of the increasing number of Palace employees. A new school was built in Tennis Court Lane in 1877 when the Bakehouse was demolished and this remained for the next seventy-eight years by which time most of the children came from the village and the surrounding area. Traffic problems arose; forty-two stage coaches travelled daily between London and the King's Arms. Hampton Court bridge was often blocked with vehicles of all sorts. The railway carried more visitors in 1849, when Hampton Court station was opened on the other side of the river.

It was only to be expected that, as the one place in the country open on Sundays for the relaxation of the public, the opening of the Palace roused the ire of the Protectors of the Sabbath. The Sabbatarians claimed that Hampton Court had become a hell upon earth on Sundays and gave vent to their feelings by writing letters to *The Times* and protesting to

The King's Arms with coach and travellers with a cow as a curious bystander.
The collection of John Sheaf

Queen Victoria herself, but a quiet determination on the part of the authorities, doubtless aided by Mr Edward Jesse, kept the Palace open.

The reign of Queen Victoria saw the demolition of a number of very old buildings to the west of the Palace. The old Toy Inn, which had almost certainly been a successor of the victualling houses of Henry VIII's time, had become derelict by 1840, when it was demolished together with the stables and coach houses. After much discussion the site chosen for the rebuilding of the Toy Inn was the Office of Works building, which was put up in 1690 and demolished in 1835. The New Toy Inn eventually became the site of the present Rotary Court. The Chequers Inn reverted to the house of the Mewskeeper by 1850. Possibly the opening of the Cardinal Wolsey took custom away.

The first lessee of the New Toy Inn, Mr G. W. Newton, was a builder and he put forward ambitious plans for developing all the land remaining in the King's Meadow. One of the houses on the road to Hampton was to be a cottage for his own use, now called Riverside Cottage. Of the remainder, only two of the proposed quite large houses were built about 1840. One was called High Elms, later changed to Hampton Lodge. The other, first called Rose Bank and then River Holme, was pulled down in the 1970s.

By 1853 street lamps lit the village at night and the lamplighter became a familiar figure. The Hampton Court United Gas Company had been formed the previous year to supply gas to the surrounding communities. The new lamps were lit from sunset to sunrise but only during the six winter months. Even in winter, the lamps were not lit for five nights in each month at about full moon when moonlight was considered good enough to light the streets. In summer, most people were expected to be home by dark.

The Houses of Offices in Outer Green Court, some of the first buildings to be added to the Palace by Henry VIII in 1529, were also in a very bad state of repair by 1840 and the Queen gave orders for them to be pulled down as soon as they were vacated by the 'grace and favour' tenants then occupying them. The decision was, however, overlooked and new tenants were installed after the patching up of the buildings. It is interesting to discover that in those class-conscious times of the Victorian age, the dowagers who moved to these apartments lived cheek by jowl with, at various times, a baker, two laundresses, a journeyman carpenter, a journeyman gardener, the widows of a carpenter and a bricklayer, and two superannuated male servants.

Rose Cottage was once home to the actress, Ellen Terry. It was later rebuilt. The collection of John Sheaf

When one of the occupants vacated his apartment in 1853 the memorandum of 1840 was recalled and the decision to demolish the buildings as soon as they became vacant was reiterated. It was not until 1867 that an opportunity for pulling down a group of the buildings occurred. This left one building, that which was occupied by Lady Seaford, widow of Admiral Sir Thomas Masterman Hardy, Nelson's brother officer and his Flag Captain on the *Victory* who was on the deck with Nelson when he died at the Battle of Trafalgar in 1805. Admiral Hardy died in 1839 and his widow married Lord Seaford a year later. It was not until her death in 1879 that the last part of the Houses of Offices Without the Base

Court was demolished, leaving a wide open space on the south side of the Outer Green Court.

The village now had more shops and inns which supplied the visitors to the Palace and Parks as well as the growing population. A grocery, a butcher's shop, a dairy and a refreshment house occupied buildings on the north-east side of the Hampton Court Road. In 1873 the Post Office was moved to the house called Oldways which was eventually to have the first telephone exchange in the village. By 1899 an employment agency for servants had been set up.

In 1880 residents could count a glamorous actress among their number when Ellen Terry moved to Rose Cottage with her two children who played in the Palace grounds. Already famed for her appearances on the London stage, she must have been seen as an exotic addition to village life and gossip.

Ever since the arrival of the Cavalry in the reign of George III a new lease of life had been brought to Hampton Court, though it was not always a mode of life welcomed by the more staid inhabitants to judge by their reaction to the appearance of the ladies who used to frequent the area around the Trophy Gates near the entrance to the barracks. In general the populace got on well with the soldiers. Dances were arranged for all and sundry at the barracks every Christmas and grand balls were held at the Greyhound Hotel (now the Lion Gate Hotel) to say farewell whenever a detachment was posted away.

Inevitably the activities of the military increased in time of war. During the Crimean War in 1854 part of the grazing area on The Green was turned over to the Army for training troop horses.

The last royal person to live in Hampton Court Palace was a descendant of George II. Princess Fredrika of Hanover moved to a 'grace and favour' apartment with her husband, Baron von Pawel Rammingen, in 1880. The Princess willingly took part in neighbourly occasions and could often be found attending charity events and bazaars. Her readiness to make friends did not gain approval from her fellow residents at the Palace. They were shocked to the core when she invited a shopkeeper from Kingston to one of her grand dinner parties.

The wealthier residents pursued a very vigorous social life in the latter half of the nineteenth century. Within the Palace there were frequent theatrical performances in the Oak Room. Outside the Palace, dinners and balls were organised to celebrate various occasions – Christmas, Easter, the arrival or departure of a detachment of cavalry or a royal wedding. The painting by Camille Pissarro of 1890 shows a cricket match on The Green. Towards the end of the century there were the entertainments provided for several hundreds at a time by Mr and Mrs de Wette at Hampton Court House, entertainments of an extravagance unlikely to be seen again.

Such conviviality was not confined to the gentry. Two venison dinners were held each year, following a custom started by the Duke of Clarence in 1821, when a buck and a doe alternately were culled from Bushy Park. One of the venison dinners was for the tradesmen of Hampton Wick and Hampton Court, and the other, about Christmas time, was for the aged and deserving poor. (Hampton had its own venison dinner.) The Lodge of Harmony formed at the Toy Inn in George III's time, and other masonic lodges, continued

Hampton Court railway station with the second bridge. Thousands travelled by train to cross the bridge to the Palace. The toll booth for the bridge can be seen outside the station and the Mitre is on the opposite bank

to meet regularly at the Mitre. Choir suppers were held at the Greyhound and the annual dinners of the Palace Fire Brigade at the Mitre. There were also the Colting Suppers held at the Cardinal Wolsey for the stable employees of the gentry.

Many clubs and societies in the Metropolitan area had annual outings to Hampton Court with a visit to the Palace or a game of cricket on The Green, followed by a dinner or supper at one of the inns; and then, as now, people flocked to Hampton Court Green in their thousands on Bank Holidays.

They came down by all forms of transport, wagonettes, vans and carts. As the *Surrey Comet* reported on Whit Monday at Hampton Court in 1864:

Vast numbers came by rail . . . As great a variety of conveyance was exhibited as on any Derby day. Everything that could run on wheels and many things that threatened to run off their wheels were to be seen, all crammed to the utmost and the interstices between the grown-ups were filled with babies and children.

The day-trippers were given a wide choice of entertainment. Food and drink there was in plenty at the stalls which lined the south-east end of The Green and costermongers did a roaring trade in cold meats, whelks, shrimps, gingerbread, sherbet and ices. There were quacks selling cures for rheumatism, headache and toothache and vendors of paper hats, artificial noses and moustaches and penny trumpets. Then there was all the fun of the fair; fortune-tellers, test-your-strength machines, a fire-eater, organ grinders, brass bands, accordion players and fiddlers to provide the music for dancing which, apart from kiss-in-the-ring, was said to be the most popular sport.

The popularity of a day at Hampton Court for the working people of London was well known. Writing in 1858, Anthony Trollope refers to 'Hampton Court, that well-loved resort of cockneydom' in his novel *The Three Clerks*.

Neither soberly dressed nor always soberly behaved, the day-tripper to Hampton Court did not meet with universal approval in the village. By then, as many as thirty extra police were needed to control the crowds and the Spelthorne magistrates used to hold special sittings at Hampton to deal with the pickpockets, tricksters and other disturbers of the peace.

In March 1873 a letter in *The Times* headed 'Hampton Court Green' referred to the

The Cardinal Wolsey Inn lined with staff and a variety of slot machines. The collection of John Sheaf

'tens of thousands of the smoke-begrimed toilers of London . . . who indulge without let or hindrance in kiss-in-the-ring and the various other amusements which used to characterise the long-suppressed fairs of the metropolis' and the writer goes on to draw attention to the fact that as The Green is free from supervision of the Park Constables 'it may be the centre of scenes and practices such as all who desire the respectability of the neighbourhood would be glad to co-operate in preventing'.

Shortly afterwards, the Board of Works introduced regulations requiring intending stall-holders to obtain permits from the police. On Whit Monday of that year the Commissioner of Works himself, Mr Ayrton, came down to Hampton Court to keep an eye on things. The newly launched *Richmond and Twickenham Times* reported in its first edition that the day 'ended peaceably and pleasantly, a testimony to the good sense and order which governs the masses in search of enjoyment'. Two years later the *Surrey Comet* was able to report an improvement in behaviour and fewer cases of intoxication.

The Rover safety cycle, 1855

There was a serious riot in 1879 when about 500 excursionists, identified as 'costermongers from Peckham', picked a fight outside the Cardinal Wolsey which then moved on to the Mitre.

It was subdued at the cost of cuts and bruises sustained by the combined efforts of local men, the constabulary and the 18th Hussars from the barracks on The Green. At one point the trappings of the Hampton Court coach were ripped off and used against the defenders. This would seem to have been an isolated incident and was not repeated in following years.

The Great Bicycle Meet took place at Hampton Court between 1874 and 1883. On these occasions 2000 or more cyclists wearing their club colours would form up, two by two, between the walls, the line stretching from the Greyhound to Hampton Wick. The length of the line was so great that orders to mount and to advance were sounded by a Cavalry bugler. The riders generally passed through the village on their way to Hampton and Hanworth and then came back through Teddington and along the Chestnut Avenue to Hampton Court. After 1883 the tricyclists took over for a year or two, but that was the end of the great cycle meets. In the early 1900s cycle meets were revived for a few years, but on a much smaller scale, and before long the coming of the motor car put paid to them.

New ground was broken in 1858 when Queen Victoria granted a house on The Green to someone with no title and no service in the Royal Household or the Government, a man of humble origins, but a world-renowned scientist, Michael Faraday, whose modesty made him doubt at first whether he should accept the honour. The house was on the site previously occupied by the Master Mason's Lodge. Michael Faraday's wife was confined to a wheelchair and Faraday thought to take her to visit the gardens at the Palace. He was horrified to be given a brusque order to remove her as invalid carriages were not allowed in the grounds. Queen Victoria was reported to be infuriated when she heard of the incident and instructed her Chief Steward to withdraw the rule. After his death in 1867 the house where he had lived was named Faraday House. This house was later divided and became Faraday House and Cardinal House.

The freeing of Hampton Court Bridge from tolls in 1876 was a matter for great rejoicing for the village. There was a spectacular firework display for thousands on The Green and a celebratory dinner at the Mitre.

On learning that Queen Victoria in 1897 had granted Faraday House to three princesses, it would be natural to assume that she was merely looking after her own. But these were Sikh princesses, Bamba, Catherine and Sophia Duleep Singh, the daughters of the Maharaja

Princess Sophia Duleep Singh selling copies of The Suffragette *outside Hampton Court Palace.* 1913
© The Museum of London

Duleep Singh, the last ruler of the Punjab, who was nine years old in 1849 when the Punjab was annexed by the British and he was deposed. The young Maharaja's prized possession, the fabulous Koh-i-noor diamond, was presented to Queen Victoria. The Maharaja was treated decently by the victors and became a great favourite with Queen Victoria. He later settled in England, converted to Christianity, set up a manorial estate in Norfolk, and eventually moved to Paris, where he died in 1893.

Princess Sophia Duleep Singh showed herself to be a strong character. Between 1906 and the outbreak of the First World War Hampton Court village found itself in the thick of the Women's Suffrage campaign. The movement had supporters within and without the Palace and Princess Sophia was one of its leaders. These suffragists, as they were called to distinguish them from the suffragettes, whose aim was the achievement of the Parliamentary franchise by violence, were none the less very vigorous in pressing their claim. For good measure a local branch of the Women's Anti-Suffrage Movement was formed and meetings commanding a fair amount of support were held in the village.

Princess Sophia put her principles into practice by supporting the Women's Tax Resistance League. She refused to take out licences for her five dogs, for a male servant, and for a carriage with armorial bearings, and then refused to pay the fines. A few weeks later a diamond ring of hers was seized under distraint and was put up for auction at Ashford. The ring was purchased by a member of the Women's Tax Resistance League and returned to its owner. Princess Sophia Duleep Singh was for long revered by suffragists as one of those who helped to obtain the Parliamentary franchise for women.

In 1999 a life-sized bronze statue of Princess Sophia's father, which had been commissioned by the Maharaja Duleep Singh Trust to commemorate the Anglo-Sikh connection, was unveiled in Thetford by the Prince of Wales.

It was in Queen Victoria's time that the Thames at Hampton Court became a popular tourist attraction in its own right. Since earliest times it had been a working river with its

Jubilant crowds celebrating the freeing of tolls from Hampton Court Bridge in front of the toll house seen in background, 1876

fishing rights, weirs and ozier beds jealously guarded. Along its length, sewage was channelled into it as a matter of course and Hampton Court was no exception. Above all, it was the vital transport link between the Palace and the village to London as well to the communities which had grown up on both banks. Now the bridge replaced the ferry and steam trains took over much of the carriage of goods.

Regattas were a fixture in summer and drew the crowds from London to picnic on the river banks. Skiffs could be hired and in 1888 Salter Brothers ran the first Oxford to Kingston steamer service. Boat builders flourished along the Hampton Court Road. One of the most striking reminders of this age which still exists is the Swiss Chalet at Hucks' Yard. This was imported from Switzerland and erected on the present site in 1882.

The small aits sported house boats moored against them which became popular as week-end retreats. The largest of these aits was leased to a renowned boatbuilder, Tom Tagg. He built the Island Hotel in 1870 which became a popular haunt for boating people and tourists. By the end of the century local people would saunter by the riverside to enjoy the novel sounds of the newfangled gramophones playing the latest dance tunes to passengers on the passing river craft. Taggs Island is now linked to the Hampton Court Road by a bridge. The houseboats are still there but the last hotel on the island disappeared in the 1960s.

CHAPTER XIII

The Twentieth Century

The residents of Hampton Court Village had assembled on The Green to cheer the departure for South Africa and the Boer War of the 1st Royal Dragoons in 1899 and the return of the 10th (Prince of Wales) Hussars in 1901. They had held patriotic balls and concerts to raise money for comforts for the troops and for the care of the wounded; and mourned the deaths of a number of fathers, husbands and sons. South Africa was, however, a long way away and the war did not greatly affect the life of the village; but the ending of any war brings on a state of euphoria, and Hampton Court Village was the equal of any other community in celebrating the new era of peace. In addition there was the forthcoming coronation of King Edward VII, after a postponement because of the King's illness. Indian troops over for the coronation camped in Home Park and three hundred of the Imperial Yeomanry in their colourful light blue tunics with purple facings, khaki breeches, brown riding boots and slouch hats with plumes of feathers were in camp in Bushy Park.

The extension of the tramway to Hampton Court in the next year (1903) brought greater crowds of sightseers than ever before. On Bank Holidays there would be as many as ten tramcars at a time unloading their passengers; and trade flourished. The public houses found ready custom and a private hotel was opened in refreshment rooms next to the Cardinal Wolsey which had been rebuilt. It was known as Cleggs Hotel and had seating accommodation for 500 in its dining and tearooms. After the Second World War, it became the Charlton Hotel. Thomas Clegg was also the licensee of the Henry VIII house. In 1906 the magistrates refused to renew its licence due to lack of trade and it is now owned by the Charlton Hotel.

Licences to draw water from the Longford River continued to be held by the inns and some of the houses in the village until 1916 although it had been declared unfit for drinking without filtering ten years previously.

For the first time since Queen Victoria threw open the State Apartments the Lord Chamberlain issued instructions for their closure in February 1912. All over the country the suffragettes were engaging in violent action and showing that they were no respecters of public property; they had damaged some famous pictures. The State Apartments remained closed all summer to the chagrin of the restaurateurs, who protested most strongly. The Palace was reopened in September 1912, but closed in February 1913, when the danger loomed large again. This time it was closed for several weeks.

The activities of the suffragists and the suffragettes were forced into suspension by the outbreak of war in 1914, and by the end of the war they had gone a long way towards achieving their objective when an Act of Parliament gave the vote to women from the age of thirty.

Again during the First World War, The Green saw a great deal of military activity, not

Cleggs Hotel. The house on the right was once the Henry VIII beer house, circa 1910. The collection of John Sheaf

only as a parade ground, but also as a regimental recreation ground for football, cricket and athletic sports. Both the Army and the Navy held recruiting meetings on The Green and all the tricks of rhetoric were used to whip up hatred of the enemy. It was on the Green on 18 June 1916 that the once well-known authoress Winifred Graham, inaugurated her infamous 'Intern Them All' campaign; a campaign to have all those with a German or German-sounding name, whether naturalised or not, interned as 'alien enemies'.

In common with the rest of the country, Hampton Court Village 'rolled up its sleeves, tightened its belt, and put its shoulder to the wheel' to aid the country's defence. Within a few weeks of the outbreak of war on 4 August 1914 all race meetings in the neighbourhood were cancelled. The Post Office worked all night to deal with call-up papers for the Reservists and Territorials. Special tramcars moved men and equipment from Hampton Court Village to Hounslow Barracks. The ladies organised First Aid classes, held Sales of Work to raise money for the Red Cross, and commandeered sewing machines for a daily working party making flannel shirts for the troops; the flower-beds in the Palace gardens were used for growing beetroot. In January 1917 the Whitehall Hotel, which had been built on the site of the New Toy Inn, was converted into a military hospital with 104 beds and remained so until January 1921. After the end of the war Hampton Court ceased to be a military centre and the barracks on The Green were demolished in 1932. The tradition of the Bank Holiday fair at Hampton Court carried on through the war years.

When peace was declared, Hampton Court Village soon returned to normal. Visitors came in their thousands again and the tradespeople prospered in the summer, especially on Bank Holidays, when the fair on The Green was as popular as it had always been. The former military hospital was now the Whitehall Motor Club and Private Hotel and it symbolised one big change that had come over Hampton Court. The horse-drawn carriages

The tram terminus at Hampton Court, circa 1906. The collection of L. Strudwick

of the pre-war days were giving way to the motor car, and car parking and traffic control were soon to create a problem, still unsolved. By then the old iron bridge built in 1865 was nearing the end of its useful life and a wide new bridge, designed by Sir Edwin Lutyens, was built a little way downstream; the fourth bridge over the river at Hampton Court; this one was opened by the Prince of Wales in 1933. During the building of the bridge the river was widened and strongly walled on the Middlesex bank from the Mitre upstream. During these works the remains of the small ait which had formed part of the wharf which had served the Offices of Works was swept away. Soon the tramcars which had been a familiar sight turning round in front of the Trophy Gates to make their return to Hammersmith were replaced by trolley buses. Permission had to be sought from George V to take a strip of land from The Green to enlarge the roundabout. In a letter from Balmoral in 1935 permission was granted with the proviso that the soil of the strips to be removed remain vested in the Crown to be disposed of within Crown lands. The trolley buses were gradually phased out and on 9 May 1962 the last one in service trundled slowly on its final journey along the Hampton Court Road on its route from Wimbledon to Fulwell.

Crowds flock to The Green, circa 1914. *The tradition of Bank Holiday fairs carried on throughout the war.* The collection of John Sheaf

New residents moved into the village when the remaining vacant sites on Crown land in the King's Meadow were filled in with detached houses built between 1920 and 1939.

During the Second World War the village escaped the bombing raids which affected other areas nearby, although one house, Rose Cottage which had once been home to Ellen Terry, suffered bomb damage. It was later rebuilt and renamed Tiltyard Cottage.

The village was enlarged once more when blocks of flats replaced houses which had been built on the King's Meadow and were now demolished. Along that part of the road an electricity sub-station was removed when trolley buses no long ran and the award-winning Torrent House was built on that land. Its innovative design attracted much comment. In the 1980s four new houses were erected 'Between the Walls' on the north part of the road on the site of a petrol station. On the opposite side five modern town houses now stand on land which was part of the first copyhold grant to Nicholas Myles in the reign of Charles I.

The post-war years soon saw the return of tourists to visit the Palace and licences were granted by the Palace authorities for fairs once more to be held on Hampton Court Green. As in the nineteenth century, crowds still flock to the Bank Holiday fairs causing traffic congestion although the complaints about unruly behaviour are not so great. The stables in the Royal Mews which were built by Elizabeth I to extend those originally built by her father are now the headquarters of the Horse Rangers Association.

The last decade of the Millennium brought many thousands of people to Hampton Court Music Festival and over a quarter of a million visitors wend their way to the Hampton Court Flower Show in Home Park each year.

During these events The Green which in the past has echoed to the lowing of cattle, the clang of the smith's anvil and to barked military commands is blanketed with a patchwork of parked cars. The use of The Green for car parking attracted local opposition and has been a matter of debate by a parliamentary Select Committee.

The impact of the increased numbers of visitors on the village needs careful management and understanding. Commercial interests and market forces are exerting new pressures which reflect in an acute form trends which are appearing country-wide. Historic Royal Palaces, a registered charity, also is committed to increasing revenue from Hampton Court Palace itself. Alongside such demands the preservation of the intrinsic historic character of the village is essential.

The Hampton Court Association was formed in 1959 by residents to act as a watchdog for the village. In 1969 the village was designated a conservation area by the London Borough of Richmond-upon-Thames. Today the Association aims to work with the administration of the Historic Royal Palaces, the Royal Horticultural Society and the local authority to minimise and mitigate the effects of such large-scale tourism. Above all, the Association serves to remind those with responsibility for the heritage of the Palace and the Royal Parks that Hampton Court Village is a vital and respected part of their own history.

The village now is one of great contrasts and diversity with a lively mix of architectural styles reflecting its development from earlier times to the present. Although the population now exceeds 200, the village still occupies the same narrow strip of land along the road from Hampton to Hampton Wick where itinerent workmen had trudged on their way to build the Tudor Palace of Henry VIII long ago.

Traditions from earlier times still have their place. The Green has its Bank Holiday fairs and the Palace its crowds. Village inns and restaurants continue to serve local residents as well as the visitors much as they have always done. Since the latter part of last century and in common with many small English villages most of the earlier shops have gone, forced out of business by competition from larger convenience stores in nearby towns. They are now private houses.

It is over 350 years since the first copyhold grant was made which signalled the beginning of the independence of the Village from the Palace. Since then, the influences of monarchs and statesmen, of courtiers and craftsmen and the ebb and flow of political change have shaped the history which has led to the growth of the established village of Hampton Court today.

APPENDIX

THE EARLY HISTORY OF HOUSES ON CROWN AND COPYHOLD LAND IN HAMPTON COURT

A distinction has to be made between the occupants of houses and land continuing to belong to the Crown, though outside the walls of the Palace, and the occupants of copyhold land which had been granted by the Manor Court. For many years this distinction was the cause of acrimonious dispute between the Palace and the parish regarding the payment of rates, especially the Poor Rate. Matters came to a head in 1705, when Jasper English, the proprietor of the Toy Inn, was assessed for the Hampton Poor Rate and refused to pay.

In 1694 Queen Mary, recognising the additional burden placed on the parish by the arrival of many workmen employed in the rebuilding of the Palace, had agreed to pay a Royal Bounty of £50 a year, and the Attorney General ruled that the payment of this bounty should exempt the occupants of houses regarded as part of the Palace from further payment. However, the liability of occupants of apartments in the Palace and Royal Mews to pay the parish rates was a bone of contention for many years afterwards and in 1839 the Vestry decided to put the matter to the test by applying to the Court of the Queen's Bench for a writ of mandamus. The proceedings took more than three years, but the judgment turned out to be favourable to the parish. The occupants of the Palace apartments still refused to pay, and when the Vestry managed to obtain a distress warrant against them to force payment they brought an action for trespass against the Overseers of the Poor.

The deadlock was eventually overcome in 1849, when the Treasury agreed to raise the Royal Bounty from £50 to £450 a year, the extra money being collected from the occupants by the Housekeeper of the Palace. By the end of the century this sum was clearly inadequate and the Overseers of the Poor called yet again for a greater contribution from the 'grace and favour' tenants. The Treasury (in the person of Austen Chamberlain) eventually concurred and from 1903 onwards new occupants of Royal apartments were required to pay a rate based on a fair valuation of their premises.

The rights of the Crown were jealously preserved as far as the land bordering the Royal Parks was concerned. Special permission was required to build on to the wall of the park and was rarely given. The insertion of windows overlooking the park was strictly controlled and was subject to the payment of an annual sum to cover the value of the light and air taken in from the park. Even today, residents have 'no right to light or air from the said Park' and they enjoy it 'with the consent and Licence of the Secretary of State'. An annual fee is still charged for this licence. In one or two instances a small balcony or grill was allowed, especially if this could be shown to be necessary to prevent damage to windows by deer. Encroachment on the park to the extent of running a drain pipe down the wall was granted only after earnest consideration, and the tenant who asked to have a gateway into the park could have been the subject of a cartoon. Nevertheless gateways were allowed in one or two instances and there was one quite exceptional encroachment (see Hampton Court House), and one which was not discovered until it was much too late (see Clarence Lodge).

The earliest houses permitted outside the palace walls were those built on Crown land to house the officers and courtiers of Henry VIII. This was the land which stretched from the Great Gatehouse on the west front of the Palace and fronted the river until it narrowed out at the point where the bridge to Taggs Island now stands and included the Timber Yard and Carpenters' Yard as well as the Outer Green Court. During Tudor times, the Carpenters' Yard included lodgings for the Keeper of the Privy Lodgings, the Surveyor of the Works, Master Bricklayer and Master Carpenter, a masons' lodge, storehouses and workshops for the carpenters, a stable and a new pay house.

The Toy Inn

One of the first of these houses had its beginnings as a temporary victualling house to provide for the huge workforce employed in building Henry VIII's Palace. When the King's new lodgings had been completed in 1536 this temporary building was moved from

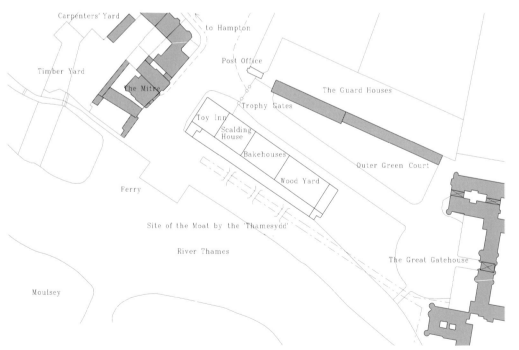

Map 3 *The Houses of Offices in the Outer Green Court*

its original position outside the Great Gatehouse of the Palace and repositioned on the far side of the buildings in the Outer Green Court where the carousing workmen could not disturb the Court and were safely out of sight. This victualling house later become known as the Toy Inn. The site of the Toy is commemorated by a plaque in the wall to the south of Trophy Gates. The name 'Toy' was possibly derived from its position on the towing or 'toyeing' place near Hampton Court ferry. What had been a temporary building was now made more permanent by tiling the roof. The Toy Inn was closely integrated with the Scalding House directly behind it to the extent that the drain from the sink of the Scalding House passed through the Toy cellar to the river and when the drain needed to be repaired the floor of the Toy Inn's kitchen had to be taken up.

Although the Toy Inn was set up to serve the Palace workmen, it later came to be used by the retainers to the King or those of his visitors.

After the restoration of the monarchy in 1660 the Toy Inn became a perquisite of the Under Housekeeper, a sinecure appointment granted as a reward for his loyalty to the King during his exile to Tobias Rustat who held it for nearly thirty years. He then sold the office of Under Housekeeper to Jasper English who was allowed to pull it down and rebuild it in 1697 as it was in a ruinous condition.

The Toy Inn (left) and the approach to Hampton Court Bridge (right), circa 1800

The closure of the Toy Inn and its rebuilding on another site were first mooted in 1823 and it was completely demolished by 1840. The stables remained for a short while but eventually they, too, were cleared away. By then hundreds of thousands of people had passed through its doors and it had provided refreshment to a diversity of customers from the builders of the Palace to the Duke of Clarence and his cronies. For nearly three hundred years it had been a fixture in the life and growth of the village.

The Mitre

The first mention of a building on the site of the Mitre appears to be a transaction recorded in 1665, when James Cragg disposed of the copyhold lease of a cottage and garden near the ferry place to Andrew Snape. Andrew Snape was Serjeant-Farrier to the Duke of Albemarle (General Monk) who had been largely responsible for the restoration of Charles II. Andrew Snape claimed that his forebears for two hundred years had served the Crown as farriers. This was evidently borne in mind by the Duke of Albemarle in his capacity of Chief Steward of the Manor of Hampton Court when in 1666 Andrew Snape was granted permission to build a stable on piles over a ditch nearby 'into which all manner of filth is flung and into which there comes no water to cleanse it but upon high Tydes'. This ditch was a run-off from the ait on which the earlier wharf had been built. Soon afterwards Andrew Snape must have started to build what was later to be described as 'a great Inn called the Mytre'. It appears that in its early years the Mitre was not a profitable enterprise and Andrew Snape mortgaged it and later appealed for a renewal of his lease at a lower rent, which was granted.

Andrew Snape died in 1691 and bequeathed the Mitre to Andrew Snape, his son who had published in 1683 a then highly regarded folio, *The Anatomy of a Horse*. After his death, his son, the third Andrew Snape, mortgaged it to William Clarke and then to his son John Clarke, the proprietor of the Manor of Molesey and of Hampton Court ferry.

The third Andrew Snape was born at Hampton Court in 1675 and had a distinguished career.

He was appointed Chaplain-in-Ordinary to Queen Anne and then to George I and

A south view of Hampton Court from Molesey. (The ferryman's passengers include a horse.) Bernard Lens III, circa 1731-3. Yale Center for British Art, Paul Mellon Collection

became Vice-Chancellor of Cambridge University. He died at Windsor Castle in 1742 and was buried in St George's Chapel.

On the failure of the Snape family to redeem the mortgage the Mitre passed down through two generations of the Clarke family and was sold on until in 1774 it was bought by David Feltham, the toll-keeper of Hampton Court Bridge. Eventually David Feltham closed it as an inn and converted it to private houses which passed to his son, William. In 1840, William Feltham reconverted the Mitre to an inn. When it reopened, the last landlord of the Toy became the first landlord of the Mitre which fast became one of the social centres of the village.

THE SOUTH-WEST SIDE OF THE GREEN

Palace Gate House and The Green

The official house belonging to the Keeper of the Privy Lodgings once stood on the site of these houses. The office of Keeper was granted to only the most trusted courtiers and it was the Keeper alone who kept the keys when the Court was absent. Each door in a royal house had a lock except for the wine cellar which had two. In Henry VIII's time the Keeper for Hampton Court was Thomas Heneage who also was granted a grand lodging in the Palace as well as his comfortable house. By the following century the house was the residence of Thomas Smithsby whose brother, William, had been appointed Keeper of the Privy Lodgings in 1628. Thomas Smithsby had been the King's Esquire Saddler and held that office until he was appointed Under Housekeeper in 1640 which was the same year that he lent Charles I £4,500. He later increased the loan to £10,000. After the King's death, he concealed his fervent Royalist sympathies for some time but in 1656 he was forced to surrender his office to one of Cromwell's generals.

At the time of the Restoration the appointment of Under Housekeeper went to Tobias Rustat as a reward for his courage and devotion in carrying letters between Charles I and Queen Henrietta Maria. He later became very rich, mainly through frugal living, and was a great benefactor to churches and hospitals. He is buried in the chapel of Jesus College, Cambridge which he had endowed with seventeen scholarships. John Evelyn, the diarist, described him as 'a very simple, ignorant, but honest and loyal creature'.

On the rebuilding of the Palace by William and Mary, Jasper English, who was Yeoman of the Woodyard and a Deputy Under Housekeeper, was obliged to surrender a large area of land. By way of compensation, he was allowed to buy the office of Under Housekeeper from Tobias Rustat which gave him the use of the house. Jasper English was also granted a piece of land lying between the Mitre and his official house on which he built three shops. After his death the office passed to his son, Somerset English, who was granted permission to demolish and rebuild the house. He later obtained approval for the division of the Under Housekeeper's House, one part, that now known as The Green, being reserved for successors to the office and the remainder, now known as Palace Gate House, being allocated as a home for the English family. After the widow of Somerset English

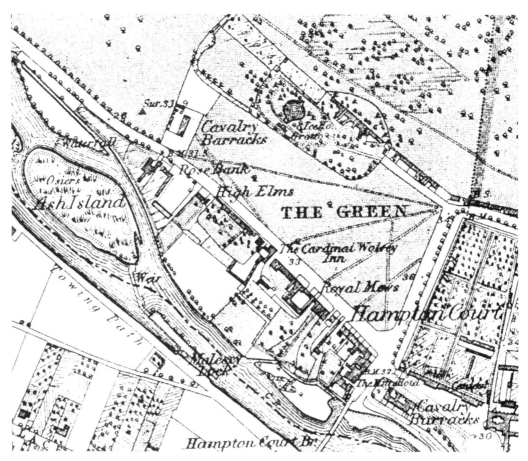

Map 4 *The south-west side of The Green,* circa 1856. *Note the Offices of Works opposite the entrance to the Palace and the Cavalry Barracks on The Green. The Hampton Gate was situated on the road next to the Barracks*

died the family connection with Palace Gate House was broken and the house was leased to other tenants, including Joel Hetherington who was the owner of the butcher's shop next door. He moved out once he had sold the butcher's shop to Mr Turner and the house was leased by Dr Francis Baker who complained strongly about the mismanagement of the slaughterhouse and finally moved for a time to The Green next door.

At the same time that Palace Gate House became vacant, two of the shops built by Jasper English were also untenanted. By then, accommodation was urgently needed for the extra police and attendants who had to be recruited after Queen Victoria opened the Palace to the public and so these three buildings became the headquarters of the Palace police, which gave rise to the name 'Palace Gate'. After the police had moved out, the house returned to private use once more, first as a lodging house and then a private house when Dr Baker moved back again.

The Green, which was the part of the original Under Housekeeper's House allocated in 1734 for future holders of the office, continued as the official house until the post was abolished in 1782 as part of an economy drive. The lease was sold to Nathan Egerton Garrick who was a great-nephew of David Garrick. He allowed the last Under House-keeper, Miss Mary Anderson, to remain in her home until her death in 1818 when he took possession and lived there for two or three years but decided to let it. Dr Baker took the lease in 1836 and after he moved back to Palace Gate House The Green continued to be the village doctor's house for many years.

Old Court House and the Paper House

The House of the Surveyor-General of the Works and a lodging adjoining was erected in 1536. The work on Henry VIII's new palace was nearing completion and within two years plans were drawn up for the new Nonsuch Palace. The Surveyor would have little reason for living in the lodging for the next 150 years which was when William and Mary came on the scene. Of the Surveyors who may have made short visits to Hampton Court, Inigo Jones was the shining star although he, too, stayed for brief periods only. When Inigo Jones died in 1652 during the Protectorate, the post of Surveyor-General lapsed until after the Restoration, when Sir John Denham was appointed.

At the beginning of the Civil War John Denham was High Sheriff of Surrey and declared for the King whereupon his goods were confiscated. During the Civil War he acted as a courier, just as Tobias Rustat had done, regardless of his own safety. Before the war John Denham had been a poet but on his appointment as Surveyor-General, which was a reward for his great courage, he does seem to have acquired a measure of architectural skill and is credited with directing the building of some of the Govern-ment offices in London, as well as Burlington House. He had a stroke of luck in 1668 when he was able to obtain the service of Christopher Wren as his deputy and to assign much of the work to him. Within two years he died and Wren succeeded to the post.

Sir John had spared no pains and none of the King's money to get his official house into a fit state for his occupation. There is a description of it as a paper building, that is a build-ing mainly of wood and plaster. At the end of the garden there was a drawbridge leading to the wharf on a small ait which had served for the landing of goods destined for the Storeyard since earlier times.

Sir Christopher Wren had many buildings under construction in various places but there was very little new building at Hampton Court Palace and it is likely he stayed in his offi-cial house only for brief visits. This was to change when William and Mary began the demolition of the old State Apartments and the building of the new ones were in full swing and Wren spent a great deal of his time there.

By 1706 Wren applied for the lease of his official house, pointing out that £341 was outstanding from his work on St Paul's Cathedral and 'setting forth the great decay of his lodgings'. Two years later the Queen agreed to his request with a condition that he was to rebuild or sufficiently repair the house. Wren pulled down the wood and plaster building and rebuilt the walls with brick. Wren's new house was three storeys high.

When Wren was ousted from office in 1718 he was eighty-six years old and had held the office of Surveyor-General for nearly fifty years. He lived on at Hampton Court for his remaining five years, though also spending time at his house in London.

After the death of Sir Christopher Wren his son, also Christopher, was allowed to retain the lease. He became an authority on Greek, Roman, Egyptian and Syrian coins and published a book on the subject. He bequeathed the lease to his son, Stephen, who disposed of the lease after two years in 1749.

Sir Christopher Wren

In 1800 the house was leased to Colonel Braddyll who, in 1810, took the lease of the house next door (now the Paper House), which at that time was in a state of great dilapidation. This house appears to have been the Gardener's House and remained at the disposal of the Master Gardener after his new house had been built in the reign of William and Mary. It was usually allocated to one of his assistants. The immediate joining of the two houses was by making connecting doorways on the staircase in Wren's house. These two houses were not separated again until 1960. By then, much rebuilding and remodelling had taken place. Of the original Wren building the wall panels in his dining room remain as well as his original lead-lined garden pond.

In 1907 Mr Norman Lamplugh came to live in the house. He filled it with his fine collection of paintings and furniture which was visited from time to time by connoisseurs. In 1922 Mr Lamplugh built a house on a site in the King's Meadow for his loyal secretary, Jack Simmonds. It was named Paddock Lodge and Norman Lamplugh clearly supervised the details of its construction as a Georgian reproduction and no doubt provided many of its features.

In 1938 the second Earl of Ypres, a noted watercolourist, who had previously lived at Ivy House, moved to Old Court House and he remained there until his death in 1958.

In 1996 English Heritage placed a blue plaque on the front garden wall to commemorate Wren's occupancy.

Court Cottage

In 1538 William Emery of Ruislip was paid for making a timber frame and ceilings for a lodging for the Master Carpenter and the Master Bricklayer. After the Restoration the lodging seems to have been exclusively for the use of the Master Carpenter, at that time John Davenport. The lodging was repaired and improved during the rebuilding of the Palace by William and Mary. Matthew Banks was in office throughout the rebuilding and was responsible for supervising the carpenters' work, much of which can be seen in the Palace today. Amongst many types of work performed by Matthew Banks's men were the flooring of the State Apartments, 'doing several things for the French Man's use' (helping Jean Tijou, whose designs in wrought iron adorn the Palace and gardens), making tables and steps for Sir Godfrey Kneller to work on, altering and moving Antonio Verrio's scaffold almost every day, and making several large stands for the Orangery.

Matthew Banks's death in 1713 resulted in the extinction of the office of Master Carpenter at Hampton Court for a time. Tenants came and went and in 1821 Sir Andrew Halliday acquired the lease through having been domestic physician to the Duke of Clarence. Before that time Sir Andrew had been a surgeon in the Army and had served in the Peninsular War and at Waterloo. He wrote a number of medical works, including a thesis on emphysema, regarded by his fellow doctors as 'an almost valueless compilation'.

Rotary Court

A Pay House was first erected on the site of Rotary Court in 1536 where, at a later stage, lodgings were built for the Comptroller of the Works, the Clerk and Paymaster of the Works, the Locksmith and the Serjeant Farrier. These lodgings were demolished and the building of new Offices of Works to provide official dwellings was begun in 1690. There was an archway stretching from the Locksmith's lodging across the entrance to the storeyard which it faced. This was surmounted by a clock and a bell which was rung to assure good timekeeping by the workmen. When Sir John Vanbrugh was Comptroller he made little use of the lodging and eventually let it.

By 1834 the buildings belonging to the Offices of Works were no longer used and were in a state of dilapidation. The Commissioners of Woods and Forests ordered their demolition and decided the site would be suitable for the New Toy Inn which opened for business in 1839.

From the beginning the New Toy Inn seems to have been doomed. A succession of tenants suffered severe losses. It was thought it was too large and superior for the locality. By 1856 the former inn had become Nos 1, 2 and 3 The Terrace. The middle house served as Mr Leifchild's Hampton Court Military college, a coaching establishment for future Army officers.

The Whitehall Hotel , circa 1910.

The tide turned and the whole building became the Whitehall Hotel until 1916 when it was converted into a military hospital. In 1920 it became the Whitehall Motor Club and Private Hotel. When another war came it once again became a military hospital until the blitz when a maternity home was evacuated there from North London and this continued after the war was over. In the 1970s it was converted into apartments for retired people by the Teddington Rotary Club and named Rotary Court.

Hampton Court House

A substantial area of The Green, amounting to about 3.5 acres (1.4 hectares), was granted by the manor Court to George Montagu Dunk, 2nd Earl of Halifax, Ranger of Bushy Park and Chief Steward of the Honor and Manor of Hampton Court in 1761. In fact Lord Halifax had already built a house there four years earlier and he applied, in effect to himself, for admission as a tenant of the manor. In 1767 he was granted an extra 3 acres (1.2 hectares). When the new barrack building was put up on The Green in 1811, a subsequent owner negotiated for the lease of the old King's Chaise Marine House which then became a coach house and stables. This addition makes up the estate as it exists today.

Although the interior has undergone many alterations, from the exterior the house probably looks very much as it did when built. In the garden Lord Halifax built a grotto designed by Thomas Wright and an ice-house and used the old gravel pit, which was dug at the time of William and Mary, for an ornamental pond. The shell-lined grotto was described by David Garrick in a poem dated 22 July 1769 as:

> So rare, so elegant, so bright,
> It dazzles, while it charms the sight.

Lord Halifax built the house, not for himself, but for his mistress, Mrs Anna Maria Donaldson who, as Mary Ann Falkner, made her first appearance as a singer at the Marylebone Gardens in 1748. As Ranger of Bushy Park, Halifax had Bushy House as his official residence. Soon after his death his trustees had to mortgage the property to settle his debts and the mortgage was not redeemed until 1780.

Hampton Court House has seen a colourful diversity of tenants since it was built which have been recorded in *Hampton Court House* by G.D. Heath published by Twickenham Local History Society 1971.

A mystery about the house is how the owners became entitled to the use of a segment of ground on the Bushy Park side. No such transaction is recorded. In 1945 when the house was purchased by the Middlesex County Council to use as a nursing home for elderly women it reverted to park land. In 1965 the Middlesex County Council ceased to exist and the ownership passed to the Borough Council of Richmond-upon-Thames. It was later used by the Save the Children charity as a home for Vietnamese boat children for a few years and it was finally sold as a private house in the 1990s.

The restoration of the shell grotto was completed in 1986 with the aid of a grant from English Heritage and from the rate-payers of the London Borough of Richmond-upon-Thames. As public monies were used for the restoration, access to what is one of the few remaining Thomas Wright grottos is allowed to people with an educational or scientific interest on written request. A covenant to this effect remains with the title.

THE NORTH-EAST SIDE OF THE GREEN

The plumbery that had formed a part of the Offices of Works on the opposite side of The Green was re-erected on the north-east side in 1700. At the same time there was a new building for Jean Tijou's smithy and workshop, a workshop for Josiah Key, the King's Master Locksmith, and a new forge was built for Mrs Elizabeth Lawrence, who carried on the work of her late husband, William Lawrence, one of the King's blacksmiths. Lastly, a shed was erected for 'old James the gardener' to replace the one he had had to give up in the Privy Garden.

These buildings were brick-built, at least in part, and roofed with pantiles. Some of them had cellars and also living rooms above the workshops. The plumbery, many times modified, still exists against the wall of Bushy Park as part of the White House. This is the only building on The Green of the William and Mary period whose location can be firmly identified. However, it is recorded that Jean Tijou's workshop had windows overlooking the park and the famous painting by Leonard Knyff called *A Bird's-eye View of Hampton*

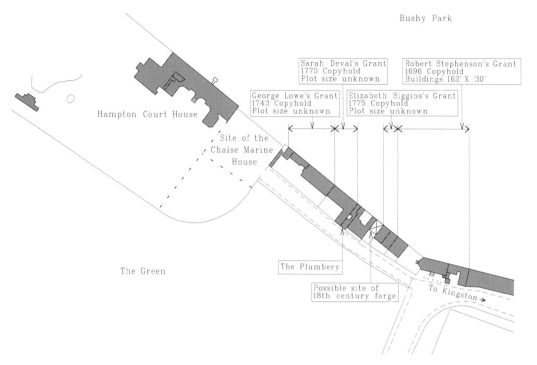

Map 5 *The north-east side of The Green*

Court painted in 1702 shows a cluster of buildings along the eastern half of the north-east side of The Green. It seems likely that this group of buildings included Jean Tijou's workshop, Josiah Key's workshop and Elizabeth Lawrence's forge. In other words these may have occupied the site of the present Chetwynd House and Bushy Cottage. It is also just possible that the shed of 'old James the gardener' stood on the far side of the plumbery – the site now occupied by Prestbury House – because that site was later granted to the King's Gardener, George Lowe, on copyhold lease.

Prestbury House

In 1743, five years after he was appointed King's Gardener, George Lowe was granted the copyhold lease of the piece of land on which he had recently built 'a very fair and commodious dwelling'. This land was described as being bounded by the dwelling and workshop of H.M. Plumber and on the other by the King's Chaise Marine House. The grants by the Manor Court, especially in respect of larger houses, were often retrospective, but the fact that George Lowe built it narrows the date to within five years.

The house remained in the hands of George Lowe or his heirs and successors for 171 years in all, though none of them lived in it.

Soon after it was built it was let to the son of Henry Wise, the King's Gardener who was instrumental in remaking the gardens for William III and who planted Chestnut Avenue in Bushy Park. The son, also Henry Wise, lived there until his death in 1778. The house was enfranchised in 1914.

The White House and Parkside Cottage

The foundations of the new plumbery, with provision for a cellar, were dug in the summer of 1700. The building, partly of brick and partly of timber, was soon ready for deliveries of lead to be made there directly from the barges. Two years later the Serjeant-Plumber, John Willmott, died. By then the house was fully furnished to a high standard and contained a large collection of pewter.

One of John Willmott's successors as plumber, John Golding, offered to serve the King with tin work in 1726 and from that time the building became known as the whitesmith's shop rather than the plumbery. The plumber in 1770 was John Deval and after his death the Manor Court granted his widow, Sarah, a copyhold lease of the house, stable and woodshed. This excluded the whitesmith's shop itself which was used for lead and tin work to the end of the century and which had its own living accommodation.

In 1801 Captain Poplett, the occupant of the house then next door (now known as No. 2 Chetwynd House) asked the Board of Works to remove the whitesmith's shop 'as the noise and smoke from the shop is offensive and injurious to the health of Mrs Poplett'. A short time later the Board transferred the plumber to a shed in the stable yard of the Royal Mews and Captain Poplett took over the old whitesmith's shop for use as a wash-house.

In 1833, Edward Hetherington, son of the prosperous butcher, Joel Hetherington, had inherited the White House and was granted a lease on the whitesmith's shop which he converted into a small house, now named as Parkside Cottage.

A well-known tenant of the White House in about 1840 was Mr Edward Jesse who, as Surveyor of the Royal Parks and Palaces, was responsible for the opening of the Palace and grounds to the public in 1838. He was the author of *A Summer's Day at Hampton Court*, published in 1841 for the benefit of the vast numbers of visitors who were coming to see the Palace, and he also wrote a number of works on natural history.

By 1888 the site of the stables and yard to the east of Parkside Cottage had a new house built on it which became known as Bushy Cottage. This has a small pantiled brick building attached which is possibly on the site of one of the eighteenth-century forges.

Chetwynd House

Thomas Siggins, the butcher with a shop on the site of No. 1 Palace Gate, died in 1760, leaving to his wife Elizbeth 'two tenements on Hampton Court Green' although when they were built is not recorded. Eight years before his death Thomas Siggins was one of the 'six poor men of good life and conversation' chosen every Midsummer Day to receive John Jones's charity of £6 a year. Elizabeth Siggins, too, was excused the poor rate while a widow.

In 1784 Jackson Golding 'of the Post Office in the City of Dublin' came into possession of the tenements by inheritance and by 1791 had built the two 'mirror twin' houses which remain today.

In 1867 Edward Golding who was living at No. 2 with his wife, seven children and servants decided to take over both houses as the opportunity arose. The name 'Chetwynd House' appeared the following year. The house then remained in single ownership until the 1950s when it was sold and converted back into two separate houses.

Craven House

From 1672 Robert Stephenson was the landlord of the Toy Inn. He took over the Mitre in contravention of his agreement with Jasper English. He was ordered to quit the Toy in April 1689 when the Board of Green Cloth decided to regulate the conduct of innkeepers. The rebuilding of the Palace brought new prospects for the inn trade and Robert Stephenson was quick to take advantage of this. In September he petitioned the Crown for the lease of the piece of ground on which he had already built the premises which were to be described in the 1690 survey as:

One cottage and outhouses and stable erected on the west of Hampton Court Green in the occupation of Robert Stephenson in length 162 foot (49.4 metres) and in breadth 30 foot (9.1 metres).

Robert Stephenson seems to have safeguarded his position as a trespasser on The Green by the persuasive reason that, by providing meat and drink for his gardeners, he was enabling the King to get more work out of them because previously they had had to travel to Teddington for their meals. The King himself went to see the premises and approved of them. Robert Stephenson's refreshment house stood where Craven House stands, facing down Frog Walk towards the river. The building stayed in the hands of Robert Stephenson's descendants for nearly a hundred years.

In 1733 the cottage had become much more than a mere refreshment house for the workers. The probate inventory for the tenant, Stephen Archer, in that year describes thirteen rooms and a garret which were well-furnished with a number of looking-glasses, prints and books. Among the large array of kitchen equipment were a tin coffee pot and six lemon squeezers. Coffee was not a drink of the working man at that time and lemons were a luxury item. Only a few years earlier the Board of the Green Cloth had ordered that, in the interest of economy, oranges and lemons were not to be used for garniture in the Palace. The 'cottage' had become a house of some substance.

It appears to have ceased to be an inn by the 1760s and by 1784 the old refreshment house had been demolished and a new house built in its place. J. Carey's coaching map of 1799 shows the house as a 'gentleman's seat' with Thomas Lane as the occupier. After his death his daughter and son-in-law, Vice-Admiral Bowater, lived there to be followed by his grandson, Major-General Sir Edward Bowater, who took the tenancy of the house after his mother's death in 1835. General Bowater was appointed equerry to Prince Albert on his arrival in England to marry Queen Victoria.

In 1843 the house was sold to John Ive, another prosperous Hampton Court butcher who had grazing rights on The Green. The next known tenant was the Army, which rented the house, by now known as Bowater House, for use as the officers' mess of the Hampton Court Cavalry detachment.

The copyhold was acquired by a Mr J.J. Ellis in 1868. He pulled down the coach house and stables adjoining the house and built new ones as well as servants' rooms, a harness room and a billiard room. Four years later he was allowed to enfranchise the property and it was he who changed the name to Craven House. The coach house and stables have now become a separate entity, known as Westfield House.

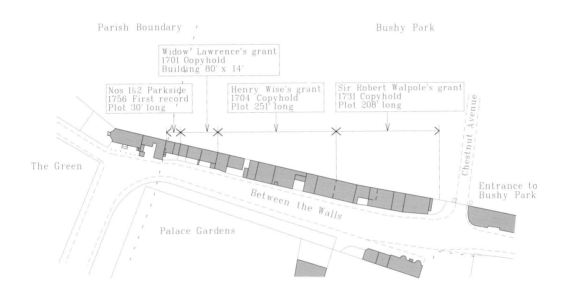

Map 6 *Between the Walls: north side – Nos 1 & 2 Parkside to the entrance to Bushy Park*

Nos 1 and 2 Parkside

The preparatory drawings made by Leonard Knyff for his painting of 1702 show what appears to be a small low structure with a high arch close against the park wall between Robert Stephenson's refreshment house and Clarence Place. By 1756 there were two small tenements on the site which were insured for £200 and ten years later these were the premises of a grocer and cheeesemonger. At the end of the nineteenth century No. 1 was a confectioner's shop and No. 2 was a servants' registry office. In the early part of the twentieth century both houses became a restaurant to serve the growing number of visitors to the locality. The boundary line of the two parishes of Hampton Court passed through a window of the restaurant into Bushy Park.

Clarence Place

On 15 April 1691 a complaint was laid before the Manor Court that Elizabeth Lawrence, the widow of William Lawrence, one of the King's blacksmiths, had built a cottage against the wall of the royal park without permission. In 1701 it was reported that the cottage had been pulled down by order of William III and rebuilt in another place. The new cottage has been shown to be a plot 80 feet (24.3 metres) long by 14 feet (4.3 metres) wide where the houses of Clarence Place now stand. The painting by Leonard Knyff shows a long narrow house in this position.

Luckily the probate inventory drawn up after Widow Lawrence's death has survived which shows that the oddly shaped house was well-furnished with pictures, a clock and looking-glasses and a coffee mill.

There were eight beds and a well-equipped kitchen which may have meant that she aimed to cater for some of the artisans coming to Hampton Court for the rebuilding of the Palace although the coffee mill may have been for her personal use. Elizabeth Lawrence appeared to be comfortably well-off. She continued to manage the smithy which had belonged to her late husband and also she received a pension from the Crown.

John Lawrence inherited the house from his mother and in 1734 sold it to Mary Hill, a widow who left it to her son Robert.

At some time during the eighteenth century it must have been altered or rebuilt for, when Robert Hill died in 1798, he was able to leave five cottages on the same site to his five daughters. By 1821 Joel Hetherington, the astute Hampton Court butcher, had acquired them. They were described as ruinous and Mr Hetherington pulled them down and built the three larger houses now called No. 1 Clarence Place, Clarence Cottage and Norfolk Cottage. They remained in the possession of Joel Hetherington's descendants until 1922 when the houses were sold separately to the sitting tenants.

The three houses became part of the commercial growth of the village and from the late nineteenth century were, at various times, tearooms, a grocer's, a restaurant and a boot-maker's.

From Clarence Place to Bastians

Lying between Clarence Place on the west and the former Queen's Arms (now a private house called Bastians) on the east is a line of buildings which for nearly 300 years have served a multiplicity of purposes: private houses, a public house, restaurants and tea-rooms, a dairy, post office, butcher's shop, offices, garage and petrol station. This collection of buildings derives from a grant of waste land, 252 feet (76.8 metres) long, made to Henry Wise, the Queen's Master Gardener, in 1704. At that time there was just a derelict lean-to shed against the wall of the park and the eastern end of the plot was used for the piling of earth and dung awaiting use in the royal gardens. Henry Wise built a house with a coach house and stables near the middle of the plot and another coach house at the western end adjoining Widow Lawrence's cottage. As the house was called the Queen's Head,

Hampton Court Road beyond Rose Cottage. The reverse side of the sign for the Balcony Tea Gardens can be seen together with shops and the Queen's Arms Inn, circa 1938. The collection of John Shaef

it was presumably an inn. Sir Christopher Wren unsuccessfully challenged Henry Wise's right to build a house in that position and did his best to prevent its completion, claiming that 'he hath built his house upon a mistaken licence'.

Five years after the house was completed Henry Wise sold it to William Cross who had been the landlord of Robert Stephenson's refreshment house before moving to the Queen's Head. Then came a most unusual occurrence, the new Chief Steward, Charles Montagu (later the first Earl of Halifax) on behalf of the Lady of the Manor, Queen Anne, annulled the transaction. Henry Wise seems to have honoured his intention to sell the copyhold of the inn, coach houses and stables, for in 1723 he surrendered them to Cross's nephew who was his legatee whilst retaining the remainder of the land for himself. By 1796 it had ceased to be an inn and in 1830 a new house was built which became John Ive's house and butcher's shop. Eventually the picturesque Pagoda Tearooms opened there; these were badly damaged by fire in the 1970s.

The land remained in the Wise family for four generation until Henry Wise's great-grandson, also Henry, disposed of it between 1814 and 1839.

From Bastians to the entrance to Bushy Park

In 1731 Sir Robert Walpole, usually regarded as the first Prime Minister and later enno-bled as the Earl of Orford, was granted a plot of land 208 feet (63.4 metres) by 25 feet

(7.6 metres) running westwards from the entrance to Bushy Park. Not long afterwards a house served by a coach house and stables was built there. On Walpole's death in 1747 his son the second Earl inherited it but disposed of it straight away to George Lowe, the Master Gardener and after his death his widow, Sarah moved into it from the official house

The staff of Togni's Tearooms. The rooftop of Maze Cottage can be seen to the left, circa 1904. The collection of John Sheaf

of the Master Gardener on the opposite side of the road. After the death of Sarah Lowe in 1799, the house was large enough to be divided into five small houses which marked the change to commercial use. At various times the occupants included a tailor, a corn and coal merchant, a baker and a saddler.

In 1863, the shop belonging to Henry Hewitt, the baker, burnt down. Three years later it had been rebuilt and named the Queen's Arms. Mr Hewitt applied for a licence for the premises but was refused as he was by trade a baker and confectioner and he had to wait until the following year before the justices granted him the licence.

The Queen's Arms Inn, now a private house, was built on the western end of the land granted to Sir Robert Walpole and later acquired an extension by incorporating a plot on land next to it originally granted to Henry Wise. In 1889 the Isleworth Brewery purchased the Queen's Arms and agreed to pay a rent of one shilling on 25 December each year for the use of the cesspool and the Crown sewer under the Hampton Court Road.

Of the five cottages, only Maze Cottage remains, much altered from its appearance in the early nineteenth century.

The Lion Gate Hotel

The 1690 survey of encroachments listed two stables for fourteen horses and a coach house built by Lord Lumley, later Earl of Scarborough, next to the Harewarren Gate (this gate was east of the present entrance to Bushy Park). The survey also recorded an encroachment by the Earl of Portland who had erected a stable and coach house adjacent to Lord Lumley's stabling to the west. Lord Lumley had been one of Charles II's favourite courtiers and was Master of the Horse to Queen Catherine. Later, he signed the invitation to William of Orange to become King. Lord Portland had negotiated the marriage between William and Mary and was given several appointments in the Royal Household. Both the noble lords had occasion to make frequent visits to Hampton Court.

By 1721 the Earl of Portland's coach house and stables had been pulled down and a single storey house built there. In 1852 the copyhold was bought by Richard Coombes who was a coursing enthusiast and organised meetings of Hare and Hounds in Home Park. Richard Coombes rebuilt the house and opened it firstly as the Greyhound Inn and then the Greyhound Hotel.

In the 1860s he bought some of the outbuildings belonging to the house opposite for use as stables and coach houses and these form an annexe to the Lion Gate Hotel today.

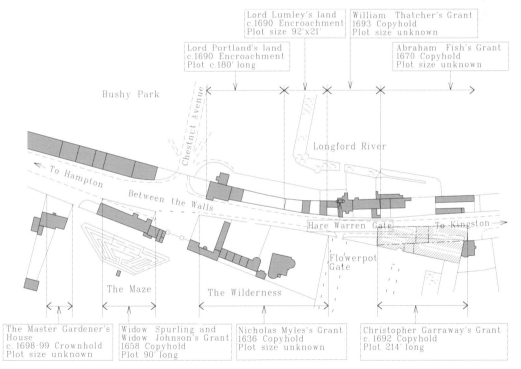

Map 7 *Between the Walls: the north side – Bushy Park entrance to Glycine House and the Palace side –Wilderness House to Flowerpot Gate*

The Greyhound Hotel and stables, circa 1910. The collection of L. Strudwick

The *Surrey Comet* in November 1889 reported a fight between the chef and a waiter at the Greyhound Hotel. Both were Italian and it is clear that then, as now, tempers frayed easily in the kitchen. The waiter, Alexander Belloti, was rash enough to criticise a lobster mayonnaise and the enraged chef, Guiseppe Banfi, retaliated by throwing a large fresh lobster at him, causing cuts and bruises. The Bench at Hampton Petty Sessions dismissed the case 'after much laughter in court'.

The coach houses and stables built by the first Earl of Scarborough passed from father to son until 1784 when the copyhold was sold to Mrs Hipperson, the proprietor of the

Lord Lumley's stables and coach houses and Harewarren Gate to the east. William Thatcher's smithy encroaches into Bushy Park. Extract from preparatory drawing by L. Knyff *A Bird's-eye View of Hampton Court,* circa 1702. © The British Museum

King's Arms. In the same year she was granted an extra 12 foot (3.7 metres) width towards the road and the coach houses and stables were owned by her descendants for the next 120 years. In 1905 they were bought by Colonel Campbell of Ivy House on the opposite side of the road. The coach houses were remodelled and became King's Chase Cottage and Ivy Lodge. The stabling was demolished and the site used as a vegetable garden. In time the land was acquired by the Greyhound Hotel for a car park.

Clarence Lodge and Gate House

The land just east of the Harewarren Gate was granted to William Thatcher in 1693 with permission to erect a smith's forge and a dwelling house. William Thatcher, blacksmith, was employed 'in and about the iron works at Hampton Court' in an inferior capacity to William Bache. The land jutted into the park and was bounded on the east by a length of the artificial river cut in 1638, now called the Longford River, to feed the gardens of the Palace.

The house was rebuilt before 1810 because in that year permission was granted to the owner of the land, Meeson Scholey, to build another house adjacent to it. This permission may have been retrospective. The new house was called Gate House.

One of the later occupants of Clarence Lodge endowed it with an unusual distinction. During the early years of the twentieth century it was the home of a widow, Mrs Goodrich, who devoted herself to campaigning against the Women's Suffrage movement. Mrs Goodrich became president of the Hampton District branch of the National League for Opposing Women's Suffrage which used to meet at Clarence Lodge.

During discussions about enfranchisement the Board of Works was aghast to discover the breach in the park wall and the intrusion into park land. When it was discovered from the Manor Books that this was in the original grant, the Board conceded that, after 200 years, it was too late to do anything about it.

Glycine House

The history of Glycine House, or a house on that site, can be traced back through the Manor Books to 1670 when Abraham Fish, apparently as a reward for his work in planting the great avenues of lime trees in Home Park, was granted a piece of land against the wall of Bushy Park 'to the end that he may build a house thereon'. When he sold it to Edward Storey about ten years later, Andrew Snape, the King's Serjeant-Farrier, was already the tenant.

After many changes of ownership and alterations to the building, it became the property of Richard Coombes in 1852, the same year that he also became proprietor of the Greyhound Hotel. During his ownership one of the tenants was Mr B. C. Warren who used to preach at the Zoar Chapel in Kingston and who used also to conduct services in Glycine House.

The land on which the coach houses and stables which had been built by Adrian Fish to the east of the house was sold and between 1825 and 1829 the Manor Books record that 'two capital houses' had been built on the site (Vine House and Bay Lodge) and also four smaller houses, North, Hope, York and Elgin Cottages.

In 1868 a 'grace and favour' resident in the Palace, Lady Bourchier, acquired Hope Cottage for use as a convalescent home for 'female servants, needlewomen etc.' at a small weekly fee.

BETWEEN THE WALLS – THE PALACE SIDE

Of the five houses formerly standing on the south side of the road 'Between the Walls' adjoining the wall of the Palace gardens only three remain: Ivy House, Wilderness House and the King's Arms. Of these, Wilderness House is the exception in that it stands on the palace side of the wall, though beyond the moat of Tudor times, and has always been regarded as a part of the Palace.

Wilderness House

Although the date of building the house is not recorded, a substantial house is shown on Leonard Knyff's painting of 1702 and there is an earlier reference to the 'Master Gardener's House & Court' in one of Sir Christopher Wren's plans dated to two years earlier. The absence of any account for the building of it suggests that it might have been done during the year April 1698 – March 1699, a period for which accounts no longer exist.

The title Master Gardener first appears in connection with Hampton Court on the appointment of George London and Henry Wise to take charge of William III's garden designs, Henry Wise being the junior partner. The accounts show that it was Henry Wise who played a leading part in this which was recognised by his being given special accommodation.

When Lancelot ('Capability') Brown was appointed to the post in 1763 it was probably intended to be a sinecure as Brown was too busy designing gardens for patrons all over the country. He seems to have made no contribution to the development of the gardens other than to disapprove of the use of steps in the gardens, holding that one should proceed from one level to another only by way of a natural slope.

Lancelot Brown was responsible for major alterations to the house when he complained to the Board of Works that 'the Offices are very bad, the Kitchen very offensive and the rooms very small and uncomfortable for one who at times am afflicted with an Asthma'. A new dining room was built with a cellar underneath.

The last Chief Gardener to occupy the house retired in 1881 and it was then decided to offer it as a 'grace and favour' residence.

In 1935 George V chose Wilderness House as a residence for the Grand Duchess Xenia of Russia. Grand Duchess Xenia Alexandrovna was the elder sister of Nicholas II, the last Czar of Russia. She and the other surviving members of the Romanov family escaped from Russia in 1919, when George V sent HMS *Marlborough* to Yalta to rescue them. The Grand Duchess was rather exacting in her demands and eventually George V himself agreed to pay the cost which was in excess of that of the work considered adequate by the Board of Works. No doubt one item which the Board considered unnecessary was her request for the construction of a Greek Orthodox chapel in the house. After failing in health for some years, the Grand Duchess died at Wilderness House in 1960.

Ivy House

The very first grant of land on copyhold tenure in the village was made to Nicholas Myles in 1636. Once a thatcher, he was at that time Under Keeper of the House (Home) Park and he built himself a lodge as well as five stables, a coach house and a smith's forge which was worked by William Lawrence.

Richard Stacey, Master Bricklayer, bought the lease in 1696. By now the house was known as the Ship. Many of the bricks in the William and Mary Palace were laid by Richard Stacey.

In 1755 the old Ship was pulled down and two new houses were built. One of the tenants was the Countess of Effingham who, in 1774, was reported to have died of fright when her clothing caught fire as she was reading one evening. The house was so badly damaged it was demolished and rebuilt. This new house was called Ivy House.

The second house built in 1755 was called the Long House, later Old Wilderness House. This was unoccupied for many years before, during and after the First World War. The house was in a bad state of repair by the 1920s and the owners, Hodgson's Brewery of Kingston, let it first to an engineering company and then to a garage proprietor. In 1937 the old house was sold to the sitting tenant, the proprietor of the garage, and two years later the house was demolished. Town houses were built on the site in the 1990s and the one on the eastern side incorporates part of the old house.

The King's Arms

The grant of land on which the King's Arms now stands is of special interest as it was the only grant of land made by the Manor Court during the Commonwealth period. The grant was made to two widowed sisters, Mary Spurling and Mary Johnson, on 22 April 1658, about five months before the death of Oliver Cromwell.

The Minute Book of the Court in 1736 describes the tenement as being known by the name of the Queen's Arms although by that date, with a king on the throne, it had probably already been altered to the King's Arms. The fact that the house now had a name may indicate that the little house of the two sisters had been enlarged to serve as a hostelry. By 1772 it was acquired by a family of brewers and distillers in Hampton named Winch, descendants of the Nathanial Winch who had a temporary refreshment house on The Green during the rebuilding of the Palace. Two years later there began a period of expansion.

The new landlady, Mrs Elizabeth Hipperson, very soon acquired the stables that had belonged to the Earl of Scarborough on the opposite side of the road on land which is now a car park for the Lion Gate Hotel. The King's Arms was a coaching inn and a plentiful range of stabling was essential for business. At the end of the nineteenth century extra stabling was built for the King's Arms on the south side of the road on land which had once belonged to the house once known as the Ship. These were next to the stables belonging to the Greyhound Hotel which had been built earlier.

Hodgsons, the Kingston Brewery, acquired the building and in 1882 the Manor Court made a rather unusual concession when Hodgsons Brewery was allowed to extend their cellars under the ground between the King's Arms and the Lion Gate, but was not allowed to use the ground above them other than for planting shrubs.

BETWEEN THE WALLS: THE NORTH SIDE
GLYCINE HOUSE TO THE LONG HOUSE

The Walls, Paddock Cottage and Park House

Thomas Mansfield was granted an unusually large area of land 990 feet (301.8 metres) by 41 feet (12.5 metres) in 1683. This was against the park wall on the road towards Kingston. No connection has been traced between Thomas Mansfield and Hampton Court Palace but it is virtually certain that he was the Major Thomas Mansfield who received £146 in compensation for the loss of his commission in the Duke of York's Regiment which was disbanded in 1679. Only a year later he died. By 1703 the plot was in the hands of Edward Wilcox who built a house there, the house now named Park House, with three coach houses and stables to match. No exact date can be assigned for the building of it, but it was doubtless finished by the time of Edward Wilcox's death in 1721.

After several changes of ownership it was bought by David Feltham, the toll-keeper of Hampton Court Bridge in 1799. Between 1803 and 1811 David Feltham built the pair of

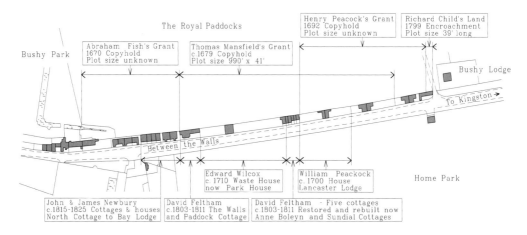

Map 8 *Between the Walls the north side –Glycine House to the Long House*

houses known formerly as Feltham Cottage and Home Cottage and now as The Walls and Paddock Cottage. He also started to build the smaller houses on the eastern side of Park House, probably by restoration and alteration of the original coach houses that used to stand there. For many years there were five of these and they were known collectively as Feltham Cottages. Now there are two – Sundial Cottage and Anne Boleyn Cottage. Captain W. E. Johns, creator of the successful 'Biggles' series, lived in Park House till his death in 1967. The coach house to the east belonging to the house is now a separate cottage.

Lancaster Lodge and York Lodge

Henry Peacock received a grant to the land at the easternmost plot of land 'Between the Walls' in 1692. He had been appointed Keeper of the Bowling Green and the Balcony Gardens in 1676 and his appointment was renewed by James II on the special recommendation of the Duchess of Cleveland, even though she was so completely out of favour by then. Nevertheless, she did still hold many offices including those of Chief Steward of the Honor and Manor.

The grant to Henry Peacock precipitated a very rare occurrence in the history of the Manor – an objection by the other tenants. In their own words:

> Wee the Tenants of this Jury doe not give our consent to the admittance of Henry Peacock for a peece of land lying on the wast in the Honor and Manor aforesaid.

There appears to be no means of knowing why Henry Peacock was singled out for this distinction. In any case the tenants could be overruled by the Chief Steward, which was what she did.

Of the many subsequent owners one was Richard Child, a distiller, who owned the house from 1799 to 1802 and succeeded in adding 39 feet (11.8 metres) to the garden by an encroachment that was eventually recognised as legitimate by the Manor Court. Towards the end of the nineteenth century four new houses were built on the garden and old stables and coach house of Richard Child's encroachment. They were named Berkeley, Oaklands, Kinross and Lynwood Cottage which later became the Long House. At some point in the first half of the twentieth century Richard Child's house was divided into Lancaster Lodge and York Lodge.

BIBLIOGRAPHY

Inevitably the primary sources on which this history is based are largely those which are derived from the Court records. In particular there is the remarkable survival of the minutely detailed accounts of the building undertaken by Henry VIII between 1529 and 1538, formerly known as the Chapter House Accounts, Ordinary and Extraordinary, for the building and maintenance of the Royal Palaces between 1660 and 1703. These are supplemented by the Audit Office Declared Accounts and by the many surviving records of the Board (Office) of Works. With such a wealth of records it is tantalising that certain periods – 1538 to 1560, 1649 to 1650, and 1702 to 1715–are incomplete.

The Court Rolls (or Manor Books) of the Honor and Manor of Hampton Court have been of vital importance in tracing the history of properties on copyhold lease from the Manor up to the time of their enfranchisement – the purchase of the lease by the copyholder – which mostly took place in the latter half of the nineteenth century.

At the parochial level much useful information has been obtained from the Land Tax Assessments, Church and Poor Rate Assessments, and Census returns.

In addition, the Editors have referred to the following sources:
Chaplin, Peter, *The Thames at Hampton,* Geoffrey Dibb Limited, 1967
The Thames from source to tideway, Whittet Books 1982
Foster, Peter *The Hospitallers at Hampton in 1338 -–Part I Income and Land Use.* Twickenham Local History Society, 1973
Garside, Bernard, *The Manor Lordship and Great Parks of Hampton Court,*1951
The Ancient Manor Courts of Hampton-on-Thames, (Part I and II, 1948-9)
Heath, G.D. and Heath, Joan, *The Women's Suffrage Movement in and around Richmond and Twickenham* ,Twickenham Local History Society, 1968
The Heath Collection at Hampton Court Palace
Law, Ernest, *The History of Hampton Court Palace,* George Bell & Sons, 1885-91
Radcliffe, C., *Middlesex,* Evans Brothers Ltd, 1939
Ripley, Henry, *The History and Topography of Hampton-on-Thames,* 1884
Sands, Mollie, *The Gardens of Hampton Court,* Evans Brothers Ltd, 1950
Sheaf, J. and Howe, K., *Hampton and Teddington Past,* Historical Publications, 1995
Thurley, Simon, *Royal Palaces of Tudor England,* Yale University Press, 1993
*Victoria County History of Middlesex,*Vols I, II and III
Weinreb, B, and Hibbert, C., *The London Encyclopedia,* Macmillan, 1983
Extracts from: *The Richmond and Twickenham Times*
                 The Surrey Comet
                 The Kingston and Richmond Express

ILLUSTRATIONS AND MAPS

The Editors are grateful to the following for permission to reproduce images:

The Yale Center for British Art, Paul Mellon Collection
The British Museum
V & A Picture Library
Museum of London
John Sheaf
L. Strudwick

Additional illustrations and maps are in the collections of the Editors

Illustrations were scanned by Project Worldwide, Craven House, Hampton Court

Map 3 and Maps 5 to 8 were researched and devised by Colin White and were drawn by MAA Architects, No. 1 Lion Gate, Hampton Court

Book design and production by Kathy White

INDEX

Page numbers in italics denote illustrations in the text

This publication was produced with the aid of a grant from the
Millennium Awards for All